The Fine Tubes Strike

The Fine Tubes Strike

Tony Beck

stage 1

First published in Great Britain 1974 by stage 1,
21 Theobalds Road, London, WC1X 8SL
In collaboration with Rawfolds Press, London

Copyright © 1974 by Tony Beck

Cover design by Ian Escott

ISBN 0 85035 018 2 paperback
ISBN 0 85035 017 4 hardcover library edition

Printed in Great Britain by
Bristol Typesetting Company Limited,
Barton Manor, St. Philips, Bristol, BS2 0RN

Contents

To those wives and families who stood behind the strikers and helped them to hold out together

Foreword

As rank and file union members we are honoured to be asked to write the foreword to this book.

The Fine Tubes strike was lost because union officials (and this does not refer just to the TGWU and AUEW) could not be convinced of the justice of the case of the Fine Tubes strikers, and secondly would not be convinced that the strike was effective.

The only way that strikes such as that at Fine Tubes will be made effective will be when greater solidarity has been organised among the rank and file of all unions; i.e. some of our greatest support came from construction workers, miners, etc.

In the past there has been no tradition of workers' organisation in the Plymouth area, a point which is borne out by the wages and conditions of workers in the South West as a whole. In areas like the South West the unions do not organise for strikes, they organise for better relations with management. And it was this weakness which allowed this American-owned company to mount what appeared to be a planned attack on trade unions. The time has come when the unions must be reorganised to fight in the places where strikers can be most hard hit.

The fight we were involved in was for the basic right of every worker to join a trade union. These strikes we just cannot afford to lose.

Hugh Scanlon wrote in the foreword to Jim Arnison's *Million Pound Strike* (about the lengthy Roberts-Arundel dispute), and it was widely agreed, that this type of dispute should never happen again: We entirely agree—it should never *have* happened again.

First Roberts-Arundel, then Fine Tubes, where next...? It could be your turn, brother!

The lessons of these strikes must be organisation and solidarity amongst *all* trade unionists!!!

The strikers of the Fine Tubes dispute

Preface

This book does not attempt to be a comprehensive history either of the strike or its environment. Nor does it attempt the thoroughgoing analysis that they deserve.

What it does attempt is an outline of both in the hope that firstly it may be of use to men and women in similar situations and environments in the future and, secondly, that trade unionists in more developed industrial areas, with more powerful traditions, may have some idea of the problems of their less privileged brothers in areas like the South West and the importance of supporting them. Of course many such trade unionists did, and do, understand this, but it is all too easy to push awkward little strikes like Fine Tubes into the background as being irrelevant and unimportant, in contrast to the more political and spectacular battles of the miners, Fords or UCS. The unfortunate truth is that the fight at Fine Tubes was as important for the future of trade unionism in the South West as UCS was for that of the Scottish shipyards. The difference was that the UCS battle was around the highly topical issue of the 'right to work', and the weapon used was the politically potent occupation or work-in. The men and women in Plymouth, however, were merely fighting an old-fashioned strike about the right to be trade unionists, like the Tolpuddle Martyrs over 150 years earlier. In 1970 this was not an issue which was likely to stir any sense of urgency among the sophisticated unionists of the Midlands or similar areas. That it was this very principle which stirred the whole labour movement two years later, and gave rise to the militant oratory of union leaders like Jones and Scanlon does not detract from the fact that it was virtually ignored, or at best side-stepped, by these very same leaders when confronted by it for three years in the relative backwater of Plymouth.

This book attempts to give some idea of how the striking men and women tried to overcome both an intractable employer, and massive official union indifference. I have not even attempted to pander to the elusive myth of 'objectivity' in putting it together, since my own experience as a shop steward in Birmingham places my sympathies completely with the strikers. If the reader wishes to see where the chasing of that particular wild goose ends up he could do no worse than read the report of the Committee of Inquiry. Its conclusions in the face of the acknowledged evidence would be worth the laugh if its results were not so heart-breaking.

My thanks are due to a great number of people who helped and encouraged me to finally get this book into print. Firstly, the strikers and the Strike Committee for entrusting me with the task and who read over the manuscript to correct the errors; my tutors at Ruskin College and Essex University for encouraging me with advice and criticism; and, lastly, my wife, who managed to decipher scores of pages of illiterate spelling, illegible handwriting and impossible punctuation, and turn it all into a legible and, I hope, readable manuscript. Despite my obligation, I must naturally take full responsibility for all errors and especially omissions, of which there are many.

Tony Beck

1 Background

Plymouth has been associated with the Navy since Drake made his reputation playing bowls on the Hoe, and if bowls has now been replaced by bingo as the local pastime, the Navy has remained as the dominant source of industry in the city for the last three hundred years. At the end of the last war, the anticipated cut-back in defence expenditure generated a local policy of attracting light engineering industry into the area, to lessen the complete dependence on the naval dockyard and docks.

Among the attractions of the area were the relatively low wages and the record of industrial peace amongst the local workers, who, in the naval yards, had not even struck in 1926. In 1945, the yards employed around 20,000 men, and, with the anticipated armament cut-back failing to materialise, continued to grow. (It was frequently pointed out to me that the prosperity of Plymouth was tied to the current defence policy of any given government, rather than the general conditions of the national economy, which was why many workers voted Tory in the fifties and sixties.)

The type of growth added another factor to the industrial passivity of the yards. Most of the new employees were discharged service tradesmen, usually from the Navy. Many of them took with them substantial service pensions which, when added to a week's wage, looked very good indeed. Naturally this led to friction in the yards, but since it was largely a conflict of skilled versus unskilled men, the management generally got by playing off the unions against each other, and relying on the general passivity of the bulk of the workers and the complacency of the local unions.

One anecdote from a retired yard worker perhaps shows fairly clearly the level of trade union consciousness in the yards in the late forties. A chargehand who was widely disliked because of his particular fetish of reporting the smallest fiddles, which resulted in several men losing their jobs, put up for election to a full-time job in the AEU, now a part of the Amalgamated Union of Engineering Workers (AUEW). The members in the yard saw a chance to get rid of him and elected him overwhelmingly. Incredible as the story might seem, the source was impeccable.

It is against this background of low wages, industrial peace and trade union apathy that the first firms began to move into the Plymouth area after the war.

One of the firms to arrive in early 1947 was Tecalemit. They had started operations in Brentford near Dagenham, but due to the high wages and industrial trouble from their skilled workers, they took the opportunity to move to Plymouth when they decided to expand.

From the first, although unskilled and semi-skilled labour was easy to get, skilled men were hard to come by in the area. Nevertheless, when they applied for work they were turned down. Tecalemit had instituted a policy of employing 'green labour' only, and training them up to standard at their own expense.

Meanwhile, a small but powerful pocket of militancy had developed in the maintenance shops of the local corporation and the bus garages. As a result these shops were being paid the highest engineering rates in the area—2/9d per hour for skilled men (in 1947) plus bonuses.

When Tecalemit moved into the area, the AUEW approached them with a view to obtaining this rate, or similar. The company agreed, in its own way—2/9d an hour was to be paid on the basis of a work norm. Such a norm was to be set without union consultation: any worker failing to meet it would be put out of a job; any worker who exceeded it would not get any extra. The union officials accepted this as satisfactory.

When a movement developed within the firm to

break this, and the union branch put up a resolution to this effect to the AUEW district committee, the local divisional organiser responded: 'We don't want any of these agitators. That's what they left Brentford for—because people were agitating and destroying the firm—we want good relations.' This, about a firm which agreed to union recognition only so far as it was implied by talking to full-time officials solely over the telephone.

Consequently, by 1950 an industrial relations pattern had been fairly well set for the next fifteen years: a quiescent dockyard, grossly conservative leadership, and a generally low level of union consciousness and organisation amongst an inexperienced 'green' workforce. This pattern held throughout the 1950s and into the early 1960s. There were occasional skirmishes with the firms who arrived throughout this period. These were mainly American companies who did not join the Employers' Association, and consequently were not bound by the National Procedure (York) Agreement concerning union recognition. However, none of these fights ever developed, as either the local union could not gain enough membership to warrant a fight—or they happily settled for agreements which involved the union on a management to local official level—no stewards.

Throughout this period, the dockyards were run down from 25,000 in 1950 to around 15,000 in 1960, though most of it was done by early retirement and natural wastage. With the local unemployment figures constantly at least two per cent higher than the national average, 'green labour' was always available and there was little if any pressure from the labour force or from the unions to raise wages.

The general passivity of the area was disturbed in late 1964 by a thirteen week strike at Tecalemit, the company which had received such co-operation from the union officials at the end of the forties. The strike was interesting in that the management's tactics foreshadowed that of Fine Tubes six years later.

Over the years the company had changed its earlier policy of not recruiting skilled men as it expanded, and the issue involved the recognition of a small craft union, with a national membership of a mere 60,000, and involving only 73 men in the plant. The company, as Fine Tubes were to do, sacked the offending employees, refused meetings with the union under the auspices of the Ministry of Labour, and attempted to settle the strike by offering to re-employ the strikers after individual application for work.

Unlike Fine Tubes, however, the company was not a member of the local Engineering Employers' Association (EEF), and was eventually beaten by an effective blacking campaign on the part of the tiny National Society of Metal Mechanics. It is perhaps worth mentioning that neither of the two major unions in the plant, the Transport and General Workers' Union (TGWU) and the AUEW, raised a finger to aid the smaller union, and do not appear to have contradicted publicly the company's allegation that it was an inter-union dispute.

Towards the end of the sixties, the South West experienced in some measure the effects of the tide of militancy which was sweeping the country. Among the bastions of peace swept away were the naval dockyards, which had the first strike in their history in 1968, and several local companies experienced strikes over union recognition and low pay (including a three week stoppage at Fine Tubes, in 1967). Among them was a strike which lasted over four months at the end of 1969 and the first months of 1970. This was at the Centrax Gear Company in Newton Abbot. Like the Tecalemit strike some years earlier, this had many features which were to be manifested at Fine Tubes: an obdurate management; a refusal to meet the unions at one point; a minority of people remaining at work (including a Labour parliamentary candidate); and violent scenes on the picket lines, in this case prompted by vicious press coverage of the strikers. The strike was eventually settled through the auspices of the Department of Employment and Productivity (DEP), who were reluctantly called in by the company as a result of effective blacking, especially of oil. This particular experience was one which the Fine Tubes management were to note, and learn from.

2 National obligations

As the Engineering Employers' Association, and the two agreements to which it is a party, play a significant part in the Fine Tubes saga, it would be useful to outline their basic features.

The EEF, in its present form, arose in the mid-1890s, developing largely as a response to the rapid growth of unskilled employee organisation—the 'new unionism' of 1889 onwards. Its organisation is considerably looser than that of its trade union counterparts, being based on a loose federation of regional associations which have very considerable autonomy. These are made up of affiliated companies within the region covered. The main attractions of membership are the low-cost expert services (export advice, manpower utility, selling techniques, and so forth) which are available, as well as the social contact for the leading managerial levels. The National Federation claims that it has little or no control over local associations, who likewise deny any authority over member companies beyond disaffiliation or suspension. These sanctions have a potency in inverse proportion to the size of the firm concerned, since it is the smaller firms which benefit most from the professional advisory services mentioned above.

The main obligation is that the member firms agree to abide by the two major agreements to which the Federation is party, one of which is the National Procedure Agreement.

This agreement, more properly called 'Provisions for Avoidance of Disputes' was, until early 1972, the structure which had regulated the formal relations between the employers and unions, as far back as 1898, after a successful lockout. It was reaffirmed in its present form after another national lockout in

1922, and apart from one amendment in 1955, still stood up to the beginning of 1972, when the unions withdrew from it to conduct their negotiations on a local level. However, during the period under examination at Fine Tubes, it operated and was used by both sides.

That it was an agreement imposed by the victors upon the vanquished can be seen by the way it was framed. The unions are placed in the position of supplicants rather than of equals. This is reflected in that the employers always provide the chairman and secretary at every level of the procedure. There is no standing machinery; the unions have to approach the employers when they wish to discuss wages or conditions, or when a dispute has arisen. The most galling clause, however, is that which asserts the right of managerial functions. This asserts that the manager has the right to manage, and this right is expressed in the agreement by the point that the management retains the right to introduce changes of work practice at will, and before the disputes procedure is activated. Should a dispute arise from such action, there is no reversion to the *status quo*: the change remains until either endorsed or withdrawn somewhere in the procedural process. This clause was somewhat modified in 1955 by an amendment which advised prior consultation by the management, but this was only as meaningful as the local association or company cared to make it. However, it might give a union's case a certain 'moral' strength in an issue which arose out of a failure to consult. It was the failure to achieve a *status quo* clause that caused the withdrawal of the unions in 1972.

In practice, these provisions are open to a wide range and strength of interpretation, and although there is some conformity within the unions, the local associations vary greatly in their attitudes and approach. This is a major variable which helps give rise to differences in the state of industrial relations in the engineering industry throughout the country.

The actual structure of the procedure is quite simple. On individual issues a worker with a grievance goes to see his foreman, and then calls his steward.

The first important stage is the 'works conference' attended by stewards and company management. It is open for the stewards to call in their full-time officer if they wish, in which case an official of the local Employers' Association must be present. If the matter cannot be resolved at this meeting a 'failure to agree' is recorded. There the matter rests until the union seeks the next stage, a 'local conference'.

A 'local conference' is not a great deal different in personnel, though the balance of responsibility is altered. The union and employers' officials presence is required, not optional, and they tend to take the prominent role, rather than the advisory one now taken by the stewards and company management. The meetings are always held at the Employers' Association offices and the atmosphere is much more formal than previously. Minutes are taken by a chartered secretary, every word being taken down 'and may be used in evidence' at a later stage. If this required procedure was rigidly adhered to it would greatly limit the flexibility of both sides, making it very improbable that a matter which was unsolved at the more informal level of works conference would be solved here. It is for this reason that both sides will often agree to go 'off the notes', so an official minute at this level is unlikely to bear a close resemblance to what actually went on.

The Central Conference, which always meets in York every month is the next, and highest, stage. As previously, it remains with the union to press the matter to this level. Here the national officials of each side confront each other, though the local people concerned may be called in for consultation. 'Failure to agree' at this level would leave either side free of its procedural obligations, and a strike or lockout may take place.

'Failure to agree' is registered for about half the cases that arrive at York. If an agreement of some kind cannot be reached then the matter is often 'referred back for final settlement domestically'. This means that some basis for settlement has been reached, but for various reasons one side or the other does not want it recorded as a precedent for future formal settlements. It can also mean that the settlement is not a permanent one, but one made while awaiting developments of some kind outside the immediate reference. Either way it prevents the recording of 'failure to agree' which is only done in the event of total deadlock.

Formal procedure has been explained in some detail here because it was the only procedure that the Fine Tubes management would in practice work with. As can be seen, it is a long and tedious procedure and many people would regard it as grossly provocative, or at least lacking in goodwill, if every little dispute had to be processed through it. In practice, therefore, most companies are quite prepared to settle all but the most contentious issues on an informal plant level basis. Fine Tubes' use of procedure could be regarded therefore as excessive and exceptional.

The other agreement which bound both unions and management at Fine Tubes, as indeed it bound all federated employers and confederated unions, was the National Wage Agreement.

Wage agreements had been made annually until 1964 when the first three-year package deal was negotiated. Although that expired in 1967, it was not until the end of 1968 that a second long term agreement was signed. In 1971, before the agreement ended, the Confederation of Engineering and Shipbuilding Unions announced that it was the last such agreement on a national scale that they would sign. (Twenty-four unions in the shipbuilding and engineering industries are affiliated to the 'Confed' as it is usually referred to. Through it they negotiate collectively with the Engineering Employers' Federation, although they sign agreements individually.) Henceforth, after the expiry date at the end of 1971, all agreements were to be made locally, and although this latter point is not really relevant here, the negotiations in 1968 have some bearing on events at Fine Tubes, as does the agreement itself.

On August 18th, 1967, the Confederation met the Employers for the first exploratory probings, and the serious business of negotiation was started at York on October 31st where the Confederation submitted a detailed and comprehensive claim. The Employers did not reply until five months later, at the end of March 1968, when they rejected it in its entirety. Further discussions on April 10th and 18th did nothing to lessen the differences between the sides, and a one-day national strike was called officially on May 15th. Off-the-record discussions continued until July 26th when these too broke down, and soon after Hugh Scanlon announced plans for a national engineering strike to begin on October 21st. The Employers failed to react and nothing at all happened until the beginning of October when the Government thrust the services of the Department of Employment and Productivity Conciliation Section upon both sides. After 88 hours of hard bargaining under a dramatic national press spotlight, between October 14th and 19th, an agreement was finally reached two days before the strike was due.

The main provisions of the agreement, and the interpretations upon them, play a central role in the dispute at Fine Tubes. The first clause in the preamble and four out of the seven clauses in Part I— 'Productivity Principles and Bargaining Criteria'— are particularly relevant, and are quoted here for future reference. The preamble's first clause makes it perfectly clear that both sides are equally bound by what follows (author's emphasis):

'These provisions for a new long term agreement... in the engineering industry *incorporate commitments and obligations on both sides...*'

The first paragraph of Section One clearly states a point of principle to which both sides are committed on the basis of the above clause:

'The unions and the Federation unreservedly agree that there is an urgent and continuing necessity...for the productive resources and the manpower of the industry to be deployed and used more efficiently.'

Paragraph two, quoted in full, leaves little doubt as to the responsibilities of the Federation and its constituent associations, and becomes central to the unions' case at Fine Tubes:

'For its part, the Federation, through its constituent associations, undertakes to have its members continue their efforts to initiate improvements in productivity, such initiatives to be based on the fullest consultations with the workers concerned and their representatives.'

Paragraph three returns the compliment from the union side, and is equally unambiguous:

'Accordingly, the unions individually and collectively accept and undertake to ensure that at all levels their members accept all appropriate and recognised techniques for analysing or evaluating methods of production, as ways in which the task of improving efficiency and wages can be tackled effectively at domestic level. The unions also undertake to co-operate fully in the elimination of impediments to the efficient utilisation of labour, which cause unit costs to be higher than they should.'

There is, of course, just one problem with the two above paragraphs, which the Fine Tubes stewards were to discover. The workers who benefit most from these clauses are those in the most inefficient companies, where, for one reason or another 'restrictive' or 'protected' practices abound to be 'sold' for productivity deals. In any case, where production is dictated not by effort of the workers but by the technology involved in the work process, as at Fine Tubes, then such deals are somewhat pointless.

Paragraph five gives the unions only two let-outs of any kind:

'The parties agree that improvements in pay and conditions at domestic level may be made provided that there is a measured increase in labour productivity or efficiency to which the efforts of the workers concerned have contributed. The only exceptions to these requirements may be made in the following circumstances:

(i) new...wage structures...on a properly job-evaluated basis, may be agreed and introduced.

(ii) where the wages paid to an individual or groups of individuals are found to be out of line with prevailing wage patterns in the establishment concerned, adjustments may be made provided... that such adjustments will not lead to consequential claims.'

Just to ensure that there is no doubt about how to handle disagreements, paragraph six demands that:

'Every attempt will be made to reach agreements through domestic discussions but, if agreement cannot be reached, the parties accept...the procedural obligation imposed on both sides in...the (York) Procedural Agreement...'

There can be no doubt here that both signatories saw domestic discussion, mentioned previously in paragraphs two and three, as being central to the effective operation of the principles outlined in the preamble and paragraph one.

3 Fine Tubes—early years

The history of Fine Tubes prior to its arrival in Plymouth is fairly brief and unspectacular. It was established during the war as a division of Moray Engineering Ltd in London. The man who took the company to Plymouth, Malcolm Rowe, joined the firm in 1945 and became managing director in 1950. By 1952 he and his family controlled Moray Engineering Ltd, and a year later, in September 1953, they sold out to Superior Tubes of Norristown, Pennsylvania, though Rowe retained a personal holding of twenty per cent. He remained managing director and was responsible for the company's move to larger premises in Surbiton soon after.

The American company appears to have taken the view from the start that it would not interfere with the British management, apparently recognising that local people understand local conditions better than they could expect to do. Consequently Superior Tubes has remained very much in the background of Fine Tubes' affairs except for a brief period in 1966/67.

In 1960, the company applied for and got a £230,000 loan from the Board of Trade to build a new factory in Plymouth. Early in 1962 they moved to the Crownhill Works in the Eastover Industrial Estate, Plymouth, taking some twenty supervisors and foremen with them, as well as their senior management.

Fine Tubes was not an entirely typical newcomer to 'Little America'—as Eastover is known locally. Although it was American owned, as are most of the firms on the estate, it was British managed, and it joined the local Engineering Employers' Association. In this latter respect it was very much in a minority, as most of the American firms in the area, which made up about three quarters of light engineering industry in Plymouth, appear to have chosen to remain outside the Association. One can only presume, in view of the advantages of membership, especially for smaller companies, that they were unprepared to commit themselves to the two national agreements. Certainly, none of them were unionised, and many were to resist fiercely any attempt to organise their workforce.

Fine Tubes, as the name implies, manufactures special high-quality tubing for a large range of products, from hypodermic needles to hydraulic tubing for the Concorde, and nuclear fuel cans. The factory does not make its own tubing, but buys basic gauges and steel alloy tubes from the larger steel plants in Yorkshire, and treats them in a number of ways by heat and chemicals.

The job process gives rise to a wide range of working conditions in the plant, from the heat of the furnaces, the chemical fumes of the 'pickle' shop and the manual work on the draw benches, to the clean high-precision work of the electronic test benches where the material is checked by a variety of highly sophisticated machines. These are the basic processes in the plant, apart from the obvious stores and packing departments. Clearly, then, some jobs are dirty or dangerous, and others sufficiently skilled to require more than basic training.

The company is the only one in this country to specialise in this kind of product, or to offer such a wide range, though other firms produce limited ranges of similar but inferior quality products. There are indications that Fine Tubes holds a monopoly in some fields, especially in the aircraft industry.

Six months before the company started production, thirty or forty people were taken on to install machinery and train for production work. Among the first to start was Dick Williams, who was to figure prominently in the events of the next ten years. Williams—a local man, born and bred—was over forty when he started as a local driver and relief worker. He had been a long-distance tanker driver, which he had given up for more static work. He took the chance of a job at Fine Tubes, as did many others then, because it was paying wages more than 6d an hour above the local average for similar work.

In view of his later role in the building of the TGWU it is worth noting that he had never previously been anything but a card-holder in his previous jobs, though he has always been a strong Labour Party supporter.

It became clear, about a year after production began in September 1962, that the high wages originally offered by Fine Tubes were simply a lure to recruit a labour force. By late 1963, wages in the area were catching up fast, and the management made it clear that it had no policy which involved them paying higher than average wages.

It was this, along with the deterioration of conditions within the factory which led Dick Williams to start thinking in terms of organising a union, some eighteen months after he had begun work there. He fairly quickly found about a dozen fellow workers who had retained trade union membership from previous jobs, as he had done.

His own words tell the story of the next six months:

'When we started sounding out people to join the union, we quickly came up against the foremen. These were people who had come down from London where there had been no trade unions and the management had apparently been against them. We came to a point where a couple of the lads were threatened by a foreman that if they were seen to be recruiting for the union they would be 'up the road'. So what we had to do was approach people behind the scenes. We'd got two fellows in as 'collectors'—one was up in the stores. That was a good place to recruit from as well, because everyone had to go there some time. Anyway, this lad got called into the office by the management about trying to organise, and he was threatened with the sack.

Once the management realised we were beginning to get organised they must have told the foremen that it had to be stopped, because after that you had to hide behind a wall to talk to anybody, let alone collect the money. They really tried to stamp down on it. Still, we increased it until we got to a point where we had a membership of over thirty-five out of about eighty, so we called the officials in and told them we wanted recognition.'

At this point the workers' troubles should have been over, or at least reduced. Fine Tubes, as an affiliate of the West of England Engineering Employers' Association, was obliged to recognise any union recognised by the National Federation under the terms of the National Procedure Agreement (Section One, paragraph 3). Nevertheless, what should have been a domestic formality, taking a few days, dragged out into six months of argument between union officials and the management. Eventually the matter was only settled by the West of England Association insisting that the company honour its commitments as a member.

No sooner had the union been recognised and Dick Williams and Jack McQuade (for the AUEW) elected as stewards, than the management moved to undermine them. They called a meeting of the manual workers and told them that the existing 'Works Council' machinery would continue, and advised them to use this on all matters other than wages. To establish an 'official' reason for the meeting they also announced the terms of the new wage agreement which had just been signed at York.

The 'Works Council', which had been set up a year earlier, when the first threats had been made to those organising the union, is a common institution in non-union or weakly organised firms. It is generally recognised in the trade union movement as the forum of a paternalist management and a subservient workforce. In the view of the union members, the meeting was clearly called to discourage further recruitment, and to undermine the stewards by restricting their role to purely financial matters. Even that role was implicitly undermined by the announcement of the

25

new National Wage Agreement, which showed that union membership was unnecessary to get the nationally negotiated rises. The only concession the company made was to allow the stewards to stand for elections onto the Works Council, in their capacity as union representatives.

The union, then, had won the principle of recognition, but what it was worth as far as the company was concerned was to be seen in the following months and years.

The enlarged Works Council rapidly proved to be a waste of time, and the company's harassment of the leading trade union members continued. In the factory, though new, conditions had begun to deteriorate. Face masks, issued in the fume-ridden pickle shop, were removed after the installation of an almost useless air cleaner; soon afterwards, the milk ration, issued to the same workers to compensate for the dust, was also withdrawn.

Attempts to raise this and similar issues were made at the Works Council, but as Dick Williams said later:

'It was an absolute sham. The chairman was the production manager, but he had no authority to give an answer to anything. It didn't matter what we asked, it always had to be put back to the next meeting so he could go "upstairs"...If you ever did get an answer, it was always "no", so it didn't make much difference in any case...All we (the stewards) were doing was taking part in a sham as a front for the management...'

Eventually he and Jack McQuade resigned.

Meanwhile, conditions deteriorated further, to the point where serious accidents were happening and nothing much being done. A typical situation was that on the tube-drawing benches, where tubing was drawn longer than the actual bench so it came out into the walkways. There was supposed to be a lookout man at the end of the bench, but the number of men on each one was reduced to one operator, with no one to keep watch. Eventually, a man walking past was nearly killed when he was hit in the stomach by one of these tubes. Another had one through his leg, and a third nearly lost his arm.

The stewards were never informed when the government safety inspectors came around. Nevertheless, Williams eventually cornered one by accident and began to explain the company's quick-change act with manning and safety shields; he had not had more than a few words when the shop manager came over and peremptorily ordered him back to work. The inspector took exception to this attitude and insisted on speaking to both Williams and McQuade.

Safety then improved significantly for a while, but the firm never did anything voluntarily. Always it was a battle for the stewards, and often a thankless one, for the company nevertheless presented any improvements as the product of the Works Council, or their own benevolence.

In 1966 Malcolm Rowe, managing director since 1953, died, and for the first time Superior Tubes intervened directly by sending over Richard Russell from the Pennsylvania plant to take over—presumably while a suitable British manager was found. Under his reign things got even worse. He rapidly alienated even his colleagues with his blustering manner, and all he could talk about was increasing efficiency. His proclamation to the stewards was: 'Give me a bigger cake, and you guys'll get bigger slices.' So often did he make this remark, to each and every question, that it became the joke of the factory. Now Rowe was dead, any remnants of personal loyalty to the company soon died and, by 1967, the factory was over fifty per cent organised.

In the spring of 1967 (March 14th), Harold Lobb, the district TGWU official, had an informal meeting with Mr Daudgee, a director of Fine Tubes, to discuss the implementation of the final stage of the 1964 national agreement which fell due that year. The deal provided for a raise of 5/- per week for skilled workers and 4/6 per week for semi-skilled and production workers, to be implemented on July 3rd. However, a verbal understanding was reached that the 4/6 rate would also be paid at 5/- on the basis of continuing negotiations for a revised wages structure. Running parallel to these talks, there were also negotiations being conducted with a view to setting up a Works Committee to replace the non-union Works Council, and also for a domestic procedure agreement to deal with minor issues. (A Works Committee consists of shop stewards on the employees' side and management-appointed representatives on the other. Such committees often deal with informal domestic bargaining, though usually within a domestic procedure agreement. No non-trade-unionists are involved as stewards are of course union members.) These talks had been dragging on for some months. Furthermore, a number of minor issues, which management were refusing to discuss with the stewards but which would make the unions look foolish if taken to procedure, were creating a lot of bad feeling in the factory.

It was mainly to deal with these petty issues and the domestic procedure question that a special meeting was called on July 8th. However, before the meeting got underway, the stewards raised a question about two company notices which had appeared on the works notice-board over the last ten days. These stated that the rise would take effect at the two different rates, contrary to the promise made to Lobb. The management replied that the rise would indeed be given at two different rates. The workers threatened action if the management did not keep its word. When Lobb was contacted he advised to hold back any action until the following Monday. That evening a full union meeting decided to strike if the matter was not settled by Monday afternoon. Since the weekend failed to see the problem solved, the work-people walked out at 2 pm on Monday, July 11th, after having given the management a four hour warning of their action. Consequently, it was with some surprise that several work-people noticed as they went out, on a staff notice-board well away from the factory floor, a note with the printed time of 1.55 pm, stating that the 5/- rate *would* be paid to all grades! It made no difference as very few people saw it, and anyway the strike was about a good deal more than the money by the time it actually started. The strike was made official within three days by both the AUEW and the TGWU.

The negotiations to solve the dispute took place in Bristol at a regional conference and resulted in the unions' claim being rejected, but a domestic procedure agreement of sorts was obtained. Its preamble is interesting in the light of foregoing and subsequent events.

Fine Tubes Ltd Agreement (extract) 25/7/67
Declaration of Intent and Domestic Procedure

(1) The management of Fine Tubes welcomes the role of the unions as laid down by the laws of England and the agreements concluded between the unions and the Engineering Employers' Association.

(2) The management of Fine Tubes seeks to establish first class relations with its employees and acknowledges the freedom of choice of its employees to be members of a trade union.

(3) The management of Fine Tubes is convinced, however, by recent events that its past attempts to honour or achieve the aims expressed in (1) and (2) above have failed, largely due to misunderstandings which have arisen over its actions, aims and statements.

(4) The purpose of this document is to establish, formalise and agree arrangements to minimise so far as possible the risk of such misunderstandings being repeated.

The signing of this agreement was greeted by Russell as the opening of a new era of industrial relations in the company. At any rate it was enough to secure a return to work on July 25th.

The issue of the Works Council/Committee was also being discussed around this period, and again the management's behaviour was equally provocative. On June 12th—prior to the strike—a works conference had discussed the matter and it was agreed that though a Works Committee would not be set up, as the unions wanted, a degree of recognition would be granted to the stewards by allowing them automatic membership of the Works Council, instead of making them stand separately for that position as previously. This arrangement would stand pending further discussion at a local conference scheduled for September. However, at the September conference the management announced without any warning that the Works Council, which they had obstinately defended since 1964, had been disbanded.

Under the terms of the National Procedure Agreement an employer is bound, if asked, to co-operate in the setting up and operation of a committee consisting of shop floor union representatives and members of the management. The National Procedure Agreement specified 'union' representation—i.e. stewards. This had been formally obtained in June when Russell agreed to allow the stewards an automatic place on the Council alongside the elected 'noners'. However, the union still felt unclear as to whether the stewards were being recognised as such or as Council representatives. This uncertainty was reinforced by the fact that the ban on 'money matters' at the Works Council, imposed by Rowe in 1964, still stood and the stewards had to deal separately in another meeting with wage issues. Consequently, though the June arrangements had been accepted by the unions as an interim measure, they were still ready to pursue the issue to a more satisfactory conclusion.

So, in the light of this, as well as recalling paragraph one of the company's declaration of intent only eight weeks earlier, the management's winding up of the Council could only mean that they were ready to accede to the unions' demands for a Committee which would have the power to discuss all issues, to engage in informal domestic negotiations and joint consultations, and to consist only of union stewards. The company had, after all, no alternative under the terms of the National Procedure Agreement. Or so it appeared. The company thought otherwise. The Works Council was to be replaced by nothing at all. At this, even the chairman of the local conference, the West of England Employers' Association official, found it necessary to point out that the Association would be bound to withdraw its support from its member upon such a flagrant breach of agreement. After a long and protracted discussion a formula was finally agreed for the setting up of a 'Consultative Committee'. Basically this was the same as a Works Committee in make-up, but the stewards had no power to negotiate anything and were there purely for consultative purposes. In the words of one steward who served on it, it was 'a bloody farce from start to finish'.

The stewards' view of the Consultative Committee was based on its ineffectiveness and the management's determination to assert its position at all times, down to insisting that its 'approved' agenda was never added to by the stewards. This had a side effect which assumes some relevance later. Instead of trying to add things to the agenda and having the items deferred to the next meeting, the stewards used the tactic of raising a wide range of subjects under 'any other business'.

Russell's temporary reign, however, was drawing to a close. From the July negotiations on, the stewards noticed the presence of a small, bald Scotsman who sat in on the meetings. He did not contribute to the discussions though Russell never made a decision without a whispered consultation with him. The stewards did not take much notice after he had been passed off as a 'management consultant'. They should have done. When Russell returned to America in November the 'management consultant' took over —James Thomas Barclay had arrived.

4 Tom Barclay comes to town

The previous career of Mr J. T. Barclay is shrouded in some mystery. In the mid-sixties, he was the production manager of Cleveland Twist Drills in Peterhead, Scotland. What particular activities he got up to are not known. However, some five years later, mere mention of his name in trade union circles up there elicited an immediate reaction of very strong hostility.

Whatever could have prompted this from the Scottish trade unionists, it was to become clear enough for those in Plymouth at the first Consultative Committee he attended. The stewards attempted to raise the question of an increase in the female rates, and a figure of 3d per hour was mentioned (10/- per week). Barclay refused to discuss it and pointed out that an agreed procedure existed for wage claims. It was pointed out by the union side that the creation of the Consultative Committee was expected to enable negotiations to take place within the domestic procedure agreed in July, rather than going through the whole run of the national agreement to York. Barclay replied that neither Committee nor domestic procedure had been created to deal with 'irregular' pay claims and the National Procedure Agreement was the only channel for such a claim.

Thus it went to works conference in January and on to local level on April 29th. There, Barclay said: 'We find no reason to change the views we have adopted; we believe we are paying reasonable rates for the Plymouth district'. Naturally, 'failure to agree' was registered, and Barclay maintained this view on July 12th at York when the same result was obtained.

It came as a great surprise when, at a meeting of

the same Consultative Committee in September which a year previously he had considered unsuited to discussion of the issue, Barclay announced that he was prepared to give a rise of £1 per week to the women on January 1st 1969, unless the national negotiations between the Confederation and Employers agreed on a larger rise or an earlier date. In either case the national agreement would be honoured. This rise was 100 per cent greater than the amount claimed, and, in the event, was in excess of 100 per cent of the national award (which was to be spread over three years).

At the time, Barclay made no explanation for his action, and though the stewards and women were delighted, they were also extremely suspicious. There was a strong feeling that it had been done to undermine the unions, and to stem the rising recruitment in the plant, which was well over 60 per cent for the first time.

Barclay later justified his action before the Committee of Inquiry as being due to the announcement that summer by Barbara Castle of the planned introduction of an equal pay bill in Parliament that autumn. He felt that he should move with public policy as befitted a progressive company. He might also have mentioned that 1968 was the year of constant appeals from widely varying quarters of politics and industry to hold wages in the aftermath of the previous winter's devaluation. Certainly these appeals made far more impression than the equal wage plans on the Employers at York, who eventually gave only a 12/- rise that year to men, and 9/- to women, (despite Scanlon's threat of a national strike), to be spread over three years.

Meanwhile, on the shop floor, Barclay was sorting out the militants, or at least trying to. The first target was Dick Williams, the senior steward who had led the work-people out in July.

His job had occasionally included that of relief truck-driver on local runs, when the regular driver had worked the limit of his hours. After the arrival of Mr Barclay, a new policy was introduced, whereby the company would use a transport contractor rather than its own vehicles on major runs, and the driver would be offered a job in the plant. Williams was to remain as the occasional local driver as required, aside from his main job in the stores. Then they changed their minds. The senior driver was to take Williams' job, and Williams was to be made redundant. He was called to the office and told that there was only one job in the factory vacant, the worst job in the plant, which involved cleaning up the tubes after they had been through the furnace. To add insult to injury, he was told that it would involve a reduction of £1 per week.

Williams immediately saw behind the move, and, to their surprise, accepted the job. It was clear to the company that he had not got the message. So, just to reinforce the point, he was told that he would have to serve six months on the job before he was entitled to the job bonus, just like a new employee, despite the fact he had been with the company over four years. Nevertheless he stuck.

That this sort of tactic was only a part of an overall strategy seems to be borne out by an exchange in the Consultative Committee in May 1968 between Barclay and the AUEW steward, Jack McQuade. McQuade raised the question of the way the union was presented to new employees at the induction meetings. He said that he had heard that although the management informed new employees of their rights to join either of the two unions, it also said that they were free to join neither, with a marked emphasis on the latter. He suggested that a steward should be given the chance to address such meetings. Barclay admitted that McQuade had a generally accurate picture, and pointed out that management did not see it as any job of theirs to promote or encourage union membership. As to his proposal, it was out of the question!

McQuade then took up another, related incident, which had occurred a few days previously, when a group of employees had sought to join one of the unions and had been prevented from doing so. Barclay denied actually having prevented them from joining, but admitted to having ensured that a group of workers who had asked which union (AUEW or TGWU) was most applicable to their jobs had fully understood the nature of the 'fine print' that they would be taking on themselves.

Revealing as these exchanges are, however, they are not the main import of that meeting. The fourth item on the agenda was 'payment rates', and the minutes simply record: 'The trade union membership of the TGWU and the AUEW at Fine Tubes Ltd seek to negotiate, through their officials, a productivity agreement with the management'. This was the first appearance of the issue that led to the strike situation. Barclay's response at that time, however, was simply that he looked forward to receiving proposals, and there the matter rested for the moment.

The general harassment and awkwardness from the management continued throughout 1969. Amongst other things, they temporarily withdrew notice-board facilities when the stewards began to use them for recruiting purposes, and refused to sign Consultative Committee minutes (which were kept by a company secretary), presumably for fear of having to stand by their remarks.

Nothing came of the unions' productivity proposals in the next six month. The matter was raised periodically at Consultative Committeee meetings, but Barclay never came forward with any ideas, and rejected those put forward by the unions. In the absence of anything resembling progress, despite the management's obligations in the national agreement, the union side decided to try to bring matters to a head at the Consultative Committee in November 1969.

They tabled a claim for a general increase in wages. How this was to be achieved was not formally specified, but on the union side it was made clear that it could be tied in with the job evaluation exercise that was being conducted at the time, and, of course, productivity. The management, in disregard of their obligations under the national agreement made it clear once more that a wage rise, or any discussion about productivity, was absolutely out of the question.

When the news reached the shop floor that the meeting had ended in stalemate yet again, the workers walked out, at 2.20 pm on November 5th, and were promptly joined by the incoming shift half an hour later. As far as anyone can say, this was a purely spontaneous walkout. What is certain is that everyone knew that if there was a time to strike, this was it. For they knew that the company was negotiating a virtual monopoly contract with the UK Atomic Energy Authority, whose representatives had been seen around the plant looking at methods and equipment. A serious stoppage would reflect badly on the credibility of the company as a prompt supplier, and endanger the contract.

Many men who struck nine months later believe that had they made a big issue of things at this point, and stayed out, the management would have been forced by fear of losing the contract to have come to some kind of arrangement fairly quickly. However, the full-time union officials were somewhat more procedurally minded. The following day, November 6th, they hastily called a meeting in the morning and persuaded the workers to return, on the basis of the 1967 domestic agreement, whilst the matter was put through procedure. Immediately this decision was reached, the full-time officer, Lobb, attempted to ring Barclay and inform him of the return to work, and to arrange a suitable time for resumption. Though Barclay was standing next to the phone he refused to pick it up. So Lobb was in the strange position of trying to persuade Barclay's secretary to persuade Barclay to pick up the phone and speak to him. Lobb's persuasion failed, however, and when the first workers arrived back at the factory at 11.30 am, they were turned away at the gate. Walking back down the road they met some mates who turned away on hearing the news, without going to the gate. The majority arrived after the lunch break—and were allowed to start work. This lockout of half a day was to be the subject of another union reference through procedure. Full normal working was resumed the next day, and the claim was put into the pipeline, the first stage of which was a works conference on December 9th.

A week before the works conference though, there was a Consultative Committee meeting, at which the management presented the stewards with the new grading scheme derived from the recent work study. When the stewards asked for details of the scheme, i.e. the job description, assessments and so forth, they were refused, as they were when they asked to be present at the management's briefing sessions with small groups of employees who were to be called into the office. The management suggested that if an employee was dissatisfied with his rating he could take it up with his steward after seeing his foreman. The management overlooked the small problem of how the stewards were supposed to represent their members if they knew nothing about the basis of the system.

At the works conference, although 'failure to agree', as expected, was recorded, an understanding was also recorded that informal discussions would take place at plant level, to examine the possibility of a basis for negotiations. By agreeing to such 'informal discussions', the company was to some extent, hedging its bets. Nevertheless, it was by implication recognising that the claim being made had some legitimate basis, and that they were prepared to discuss that basis. In any event, had the management been convinced that it was a completely illegitimate claim, it is highly unlikely that they would have even considered talking about it, and would have invoked the national agreement.

The question of informal talks was pressed again a month later at the January 3rd Consultative Committee meeting. None had transpired in the intervening period, despite attempts from the officials of both unions, so a joint reference was submitted, that read as follows:

'...that an informal conference be held between representatives of the TGWU and the AUEW and management in order to discuss the best method to be adopted with regard to concluding a productivity deal with the company.'

It was recorded in the minutes that the company intended to give this serious consideration and would reply at the next meeting.

If this submitted reference did nothing else, it re-established firmly the legitimacy of the claim by reintroducing the productivity factor. The company too appeared to be moving quite definitely into a position compatible with its obligations under the agreement.

This however, was not to last, for at the next Consultative Committee meeting on February 3rd, Barclay declared that he could not see that an informal meeting would serve any purpose. When questioned by the senior steward, Dick Williams, Barclay's minuted reply was that he 'did not think it would be appropriate at this time to discuss the productivity deal'. At the following meeting, the minutes were challenged and the stewards felt that Barclay's remarks were more accurately summed up by saying he was not interested in a productivity deal any time. Whatever was said, it is clear that the management was once again slamming the door that appeared to have been only pushed ajar by strike action.

The management's return to a hard-line position in the Committee was recognised by one or two of the more farsighted trade unionists as preparation for the showdown that had had to be avoided four months earlier. Those preparations included an attempt to buy out the most experienced and influential shop steward—Dick Williams.

After Dick Williams had been transferred to the pickle shop after the 1967 strike, he had stuck the job until the middle of 1969 when, by taking advantage of the customary dislocation amongst senior personnel during the summer holiday period, he had managed to get himself transferred to the ultrasonic test lab, a separate department from the production side, and under a different manager. All hell was let loose when this was discovered after the holidays, but Williams had been transferred quite properly by the 'stand-in' staff, was proving adept at his new job, and thus could not easily be moved without creating a clear-cut victimisation issue, so the matter was not taken any further.

Shortly after Barclay categorically rejected any productivity deal in March 1970, Daugee, the Company Secretary and a director, called Williams up to the office. To use Williams's words again:

'He said they were thinking of increasing their supervisory staff: "I have four names—yours is one of them." I said "Thank you very much, it's nice to know you're pleased with my work." Then he told me: "There's one snag. We'd expect you to be loyal to the company, and not to any other organisation." So I said, "What you're asking me to do is to forgo my union activities." "Well," he said, "you can be a member of a union, but we don't want you to be active." So I asked him if he was guaranteeing me a good job if I promised to lay off with the union. "Oh no," he said. He was only telling me my name was on the short list to be considered. I told them where to stick that one!'

Williams's reward for integrity was an immediate transfer to another job in the Inspection Department.

'It was a gash job anyone could do, though it was always done by an inspector. Well, just after I was put on it, they made it a day work job, where previously it had been a shift job, done in turns. Not only did I lose the shift bonus, but come 4.30, when day workers knocked off, they always put an inspector from the shift on the job, so I never got any overtime either. So I was losing £10 per week, with the others working twelve hour shifts.'

Williams's last remarks, about the enormous amount of overtime being worked, point to a strange atmosphere developing in the plant. After the rejection of any productivity talks in March, everyone realised that sooner or later something was going to happen. The management were offering as much overtime as anyone wanted (except for Dick Williams), which several individuals recognised as their preparation for a strike. Nevertheless, despite the widespread expectation of a strike, the majority of work-people were not prepared to assume the worst, and, confident of their case, expected to see Barclay put in his place when the issue got to York. Consequently, an attempt to limit or cut out overtime was rejected, on the basis that either the laugh would be on Barclay or that they could use the money if they did have to go out.

This touching faith in legitimate procedural bargaining is a telling measure, both of their inexperience, and also of their good faith in abiding by agreements in the face of the provocations offered by the management.

The issue continued on its way through to York via a local conference held in mid-April. This conference was interesting because it was the first time a third party was involved in the claim—the Employers' Association, who might have been expected to emphasise the responsibilities of both sides under the terms of the agreement. It was not necessary in the case of the union side, for they opened the meeting with their statement that: 'The trade union side are fully aware of the terms of the agreement between the Engineering Employers' Federation and the Confederation dated December 10th 1968.' The union then attempted to obtain a commitment in principle from the management to an agreement based on productivity criteria. The only response from the other side was to ask the union to submit proposals, without committing themselves to anything. The rest of the meeting consisted of both sides seeking commitments from the other. It is perhaps worth repeating clause two of the national agreement at this point:

'For its part, the Federation, through its constituent associations, undertakes to have its members continue their efforts to initiate improvements in productivity, such initiatives to be based on the fullest consultation with the workers concerned and their representatives.'

It can hardly be argued that the unions had not shown themselves willing, right from a year before, in April 1969, to talk about productivity deals. It is clear however, that clause two did not exist as far as Fine Tubes were concerned.

They cannot complain that they were not warned, for Mr John of the AUEW is recorded as saying: 'If we have failure to agree this morning the balloon will go up...' Nothing could have been more accurately prophetic as events turned out.

5 June 15th

On the afternoon of June 12th 1970, at 3.30 pm, the stewards were informed over the phone that the Central Conference at York had ended in yet another 'failure to agree'. This news was met with anger and frustration by the work-people, and many were ready to walk out there and then. Dick Williams, who had been off work sick that week, came into the plant about that time to collect his health insurance pay. The other stewards caught him and explained the situation. Williams successfully urged the workers to keep working, while the stewards tried to get a meeting with the management.

Although Barclay and the personnel manager, Chapman, were both away at York, two other directors were in the factory, but despite two attempts by the stewards they would not make themselves available. Eventually, a message was left with Chapman's secretary to the effect that the stewards considered that the situation had reached a state of the utmost gravity, and that they would hold themselves ready for a meeting at any time over the weekend. Needless to say their offer was not taken up.

At 7 am on Monday, everyone on the first shift reported for work. The atmosphere was very tense and a word from the stewards would have seen them outside the gates in double time. At 8.45, Chapman came in and the stewards went straight up to see him. A written agenda was given to him and they stayed approximately an hour, explaining the urgency of the situation, the mood of the workers and discussing the meeting time and the disputes procedure. Chapman agreed that a meeting was highly desirable, but pointed out that Monday was a particularly busy morning, and that Barclay was engaged at that moment. The stewards appreciated the position and left after Chapman's assurances that every effort would be made to get everyone together as soon as possible. The men returned to the shop floor at about 9.45 and carried on working. At 10.30 Barclay was seen on the shop floor talking to foremen, charge-hands and a couple of non-union members, presumably—as the stewards claimed later—'testing the temperature' of the shop floor. He was still there when the workers on the early shift went to lunch at 11.30 leaving the ordinary day-shift people at work.

Once in the canteen, a meeting got underway immediately, and as on the Friday, there was a great deal of rank-and-file pressure to strike. The stewards temporarily withstood the pressure with a promise to call them out if a meeting was not arranged by 2.00. They left at 11.50, and in their *own* time went to see Chapman again. This time it was made clear, with no diplomatic evasions, that the stewards would be unable to answer for the action of their members if a meeting time was not arranged by 2.00. Chapman claimed that he was still having trouble pinning down Barclay but said he would keep on trying.

By 2.00, nothing had been heard and the stewards made a last effort by going up to see Chapman for a third time that day. Twenty minutes later they returned to the factory floor with nothing to report.

Sixty people walked off the shop floor at 2.30. They were joined by nearly 60 more on the incoming, second day shift at 3.00, and another 50-odd night-shift workers made the total number of strikers 173. Four returned the next day leaving 169 out of a possible 190 out on strike on the morning of June 16th.

To hear the management version of events on June 15th, one could well believe it was June 15th of a different year. There are in fact only two points at which the versions agree. The first is that Chapman agrees that he and the stewards met at 8.45 and discussed the situation informally until around 9.30. However, he denies firstly that he received any message from his secretary about the stewards' approaches the previous Friday, secondly, that he saw the stewards at 11.50, and thirdly, that he saw the stewards finally at 2.00. He does however claim that he met Williams alone at 11.00 in his office, where he handed the senior steward a typed notice of a meeting, though there was no time printed on it. Williams was informed verbally that the meeting had been arranged for 3 pm, the time when the shift was due to clock off and a new one come in. (It must be emphasised that Dick Williams has strongly and consistently refuted the truth of this allegation.) Barclay meanwhile claims that he saw Chapman several times that morning and yet knew nothing at all about the threatened walkout, though he was told about the request for a meeting. The event came as a complete surprise to him. He admits to having been on the factory floor that morning, but only for twenty minutes at most, around 10.30 and accompanied by an important business visitor whom he was with for most of the morning. While he had been in the plant he had noticed absolutely nothing wrong.

If we examine the two versions of the events briefly, we find the unions' version stands up not only in terms of its own internal consistency, but also because the picture of management that arises does not in any way contradict the impression which had been created in the incidents over the previous six years.

If we approach the management's version in the same way, that is, to judge it upon credibility and consistency, both within itself and against itself, we come up against some strange anomalies. Firstly, in view of the registered failure to agree at York on the Friday, Barclay must have at least had some idea that there would be a reaction amongst the workpeople, especially as he heard Mr. John's remark. Moreover, it would be fairly obvious that the stewards would be seeking a meeting. Since they had done exactly that, early on Monday morning, if not before, Chapman would have surely mentioned it when they passed each other to and fro. Chapman himself did not deny the urgency of the stewards' representations at 9 am that morning, making it even less likely that he would have failed to have mentioned it to Barclay when he arranged a meeting with him for the stewards—if he did.

On the basis of the management's version, a meeting was allegedly arranged at 3 pm. Since both Chapman and the stewards agree that the reason a time was not given at 9 am was because Barclay could not be contacted then, it seems highly likely that Barclay must have known a meeting was being sought before 11 a.m. (when it is alleged Williams was given the notice agreeing to such a meeting), and that he realised the urgency of it.

Both Barclay and Chapman complained that, although they were bending over backwards to call a meeting as soon as possible, they had not the slightest idea what it involved! They offered by way of excuse that the agenda placed before Chapman that morning had only routine items on it; but since the stewards were in the habit of introducing all sorts of subjects under 'any other business', they thought that it was there that any 'urgent question' lay. This last may well be true, bearing in mind the previously noted remarks of the stewards about Barclay's control over the agenda of the Consultative Committees.

Nothwithstanding the inconsistencies so far outlined, there is an entirely separate factor which was introduced and explored thoroughly at the Committee of Inquiry. This was the question of the missing distribution list. The procedure for a notice calling a meeting was that a distribution list was made prior to the material being sent out. The notices were then posted on the notice-boards and given to each steward concerned. The list and a copy of the notice were then filed.

It was established in the Inquiry that such a list existed for every kind of meeting called in the last four years, including those called at short notice on urgent or special matters. These were available to the Committee, and one such list was produced for a meeting called at one and a half hour's notice in 1968. Although management claimed that four hour's notice was given to Williams, they could not produce such a list, nor a copy of the notice that was handed to him. Something that jars with normal procedure in any bureaucracy can often be more revealing than hours of legal debate about details.

It seems extremely probable that of the two stories, the company's is the false one. It lacks both consistency and credibility. Of the two sides it was the company, in the light of their previous record of labour relations, that had the most to lose by admitting to the Committee they had stalled and vacillated over the question of calling a meeting. Their story is thoroughly implausible to anyone experienced in labour relations—a shop steward seeing a personnel manager alone, receiving notice of a meeting and leading a walkout half an hour before it was due, after requesting it—this is too ridiculous to credit. It also tends to demonstrate that the management's experience had been limited strictly to labour confrontation during the previous six years, otherwise they could never have created such a story.

6 Opening moves

Three days after the strike began the workers were hit by a national disaster, though it was several months before they appreciated its enormity as far as their own position was concerned. A Conservative Government was elected.

On a more parochial level events moved slowly. There were indications of future developments in several incidents during the first fortnight. A picket was hurt by a scab rushing the picket line in his car. The police advised the pickets they were causing an obstruction, and liable to arrest. Ron Nethercott, the TGWU Regional Secretary said publicly, towards the end of the month, that Barclay's attitude, past and present, made the outcome of the strike significant for trade unionism in the South West. None of these events made more than a couple of column inches in the local press.

On the strikers' side, little was happening. Most of them believed it would not last very long, and apart from putting twelve hour pickets on the gate, left things to their officials. However, at the start the attitude of some of the officials was less than helpful. Although the local official, Ron Webber, had got the strike made official pretty quickly, the district secretary, who was on the point of retiring, told the men to go back to work, though such a view rapidly became untenable in the light of what followed.

June 30th put the strike back on the front page of the Plymouth press. In an unprecedented move, the management sent a letter to all employees on strike, containing the following ultimatum:

'Dear Mr...
Unless you have resumed work by Wednesday 1st

July 1970, then with effect from that date, and in accordance with the 'Contracts of Employment Act 1963' we hereby give you four weeks notice of termination of your employment with this Company.

Your employment will therefore terminate on Tuesday July 28th, on which date your accrued holiday pay, P.45, and National Insurance card will be forwarded to you by registered post.

Please note, any tax refund due to you this week will also be forwarded to you by registered post.

signed: *T. Chapman*
for Fine Tubes: Personnel Manager.'

No more positive declaration of war on conventional industrial relations—even during a strike—was possible. Yet it was entirely consistent with the general behaviour of Fine Tubes' management over the past ten years. There is evidence (from the Committee of Inquiry) that Barclay had canvassed support beforehand from the local Employers' Association but had been advised against it. He claimed later that he had wished 'to force a decision' and that he believed that this was the best way to do it.

He was in fact successful in convincing four of the remaining 169 strikers to return to work in the following fortnight. He was also successful in persuading the rest that their self-respect was at stake now, as well as trade union principles.

The letter appeared to have wider repercussions locally. Immediately after it appeared in the press, recruitment into the TGWU soared to over 400 a week, more than double its usual rate, for weeks. Indeed the strike appeared to stimulate recruitment throughout the West Country for several months, though it would of course be impossible to say what, if anything, else was involved. What can be said is that work-people in factories which had hitherto been virtually unorganisable, such as Ranco, an American company, joined the union in large numbers.

The strike committee, which apart from organising the picket, had done very little, realised that the strike was going to be more than a short skirmish. They decided to start a programme of public activity with a demonstration at the opening of the forthcoming 'American Fortnight' in Plymouth. This was largely a jingoist 'ra-ra' about the Pilgrim Fathers, balanced by an obsequious public gratitude for the local jobs created by US investment.

The opening ceremony was on July 5th (the 4th was a Sunday), and was performed by one Admiral Waldemar Wendt, Commander-in-Chief of US Naval forces in Europe. He was met by placards carrying the clumsy if appropriate slogan 'FAIR PLAY FROM PLYMOUTH/U.S.-OWNED INDUSTRY'. The noise however, was reserved for the labour businessman, who also served as Lord Mayor, Mr Eric Nuttall, when he began the expected warm speech about the virtues of the US investment locally. The noise however, was minimal, for the strikers were as yet too self-conscious, too inexperienced, to risk the kind of public scene that would be caused by a concerted attempt to disrupt the meeting, but this was the first of several, and progressively more militant demonstrations.

Their next public outing was a week later, and was originally conceived as being of a very different nature. This was the occasion of the annual commemoration of the Tolpuddle Martyrs at the village of Tolpuddle in Devon. Vic Feather was the main speaker at this solemn gathering of trade unionists from all over the South West. The strikers saw an excellent opportunity to make useful contacts and win the support of the leader of the trade union movement. Thus they went along in the naïve expectation of a warm welcome from the General Secretary of the TUC, and at the very least, some friendly words of encouragement after six weeks on strike. They took along a few placards, and when they arrived, they found a similar delegation from Ottermill Switchgear in Exeter, who had been out for twelve weeks, and a group from Centrax where a four month strike had not long been concluded. All had turned up with the same expectations.

The delegations attempted to have a few words with the 'senior statesman of labour', only to find themselves brushed off with bare politeness. This was bad enough, and spoiled the naïve illusions they came with. However, there was worse to come. Not content with snubbing them privately, when Feather took the microphone to address the assembled multitudes, he berated them publicly, and patronisingly preached the virtues of procedure and the honouring of agreements. Nor was this all, for when one of the Centrax men attempted to defend the local strikers Feather picked on him and, referring to his longish hair, proceeded to assume he was a student, addressing him personally, and boasting that he had held a union card for over thirty years. Feather ended his tirade by telling the strikers to go home, to go back to their factories and organise themselves. When they had done that they could come back and see him.

The man whom the TUC General Secretary had lectured so virulently was in fact David Ferguson who was the convenor at Centrax, and had been for seven years. There is no record of Mr Feather ever having held a such a position, the highest shop floor office in a trade union, nor is there any public record of his ever playing a leading role in a four month strike. There are many substantiated records of his having large meals in the best hotels with amicable employers. He also wears his hair short! The strikers, publicly humiliated, came away boiling mad, but with one important lesson learned, and one which they have never forgotten.

Throughout this period the official side of the unions had been attempting to exert their influence, and having failed to get Barclay to talk, persuaded the local Department of Employment and Productivity Conciliation Service to attempt to find a solution. After meeting the regional union and Employers' Association officials in Bristol, they went down to Plymouth the next day, where they were shown round the factory by Chapman, but were refused an interview with Barclay. No talks resulted from this visit.

In the Plymouth area generally, at this time, an interesting phenomenon was taking place. As has already been mentioned, union recruitment had suddenly doubled in the first two or three weeks in July. In the third week seven or eight non-union firms suddenly announced pay rises of between 8% and 14% for their workers. This was openly attributed to the effects of the Fine Tubes strike and the subsequent union growth by official union spokesmen, who claimed that the rises were 'an attempt to buy out the union cards'.

On July 25th, Barclay dropped his biggest bombshell to date, bigger than the dismissal notices even, in the eyes of the strikers at least. He calmly announced that he had awarded a 9% rise to those workers who had remained at work, and new employees. This rise would be backdated four weeks, that is, to within a fortnight of the start of the strike. A further 4% would follow in the autumn, and, in addition, staff conditions would be awarded to all workers.

It was not, however, all it appeared to be. Not only was the rise almost completely phoney, but the justifications for it that Barclay felt he had to make were hardly credible. To explain the rise itself, it is necessary to understand both the somewhat complicated shift system that was operating *before* the strike and the one that was implemented *after* the strike. (The latter was the subject of a reference through procedure at the time.)

The shift system operating prior to the strike was as follows: firstly, an ordinary day shift of 8 am to 4.30 pm operated; alongside that was a double day shift from 7 am to 3 pm, and a second double day shift from 3 pm to 11 pm. There was also a night shift from 11 pm to 8 am. The ordinary (8-4.30) day shift were mainly maintenance and women workers and were permanently on that shift, as were the night shift who were production workers. The double day shift men alternated late and early shifts weekly. Day shift was paid basic 40 hour rate, double day were paid a weekly shift bonus of four hours, and the night shift men an eight hour shift bonus.

The shift system Barclay wanted to introduce was simply to abolish the double day shift and have all workers alternate fortnightly between day and night shift paying, as before, no shift bonus to the day workers, and only four hour's shift bonus to the night workers. As this system had been worked out without consultation with the stewards or union officials, it had been rejected and sent to York. Consequently, as soon as the union had been disposed of, by dismissing all its members, Barclay introduced the shift system he had wanted.

The subsequent drop in earnings can be seen in the table opposite, which sets out the pay for a worker on *top* rate of 45p per hour, on each of the five shifts over a four week period.

As can be seen from these figures, a double day shift worker dropped 5% on the new shift system—so the 9% rise was in fact only 4% for him, with another 4% to follow in the autumn. For the night shift the drop was even more drastic, losing nearly £2 per week, which amounts to 8%. For them the 9% rise left them 1% above their previous level, leaving them to wait till autumn to get 4% over their old rate. The only workers to benefit from the full 13% were the original day-shift workers, most of whom were maintenance men, or women who would not be working at a male rate anyway. The rise never, except in the case of a very few male workers on day shift, amounted to anything like the advertised rates, containing within them a large element of adjustment to the new shift system.

The rise was not the only phoney issue however. Fine Tubes felt obliged to issue a statement that it had been given because an increase had been awarded to the dockyard workers, and wishing to remain competitive, they felt their action was justified.

The truth of this can be judged from the following: firstly, at no point in the previous nine months had Barclay ever given any indication that he was prepared to consider a rise. Since the dockyard workers' negotiations had been going on for at least six months, Barclay could have offered to re-examine the claim in the light of any dockyard award, long

shift	hours	rate	weekly basic	shift bonus	weekly total	total 2 weeks	total monthly
old system							
night	40	45p	£18	£3.60	£21.60	£43.20	£86.40
day	40	45p	£18	—	£18.00	£36.00	£72.00
d/day	40	45p	£18	£1.80	£19.80	£39.60	£79.20
new system							
day	40	45p	£18	—	£18.00	£36.00	
night	40	45p	£18	£1.80	£19.80	£39.60	
					all workers now receive monthly		£75.60

Thus: night shift   workers *lose* £1.80 per week   (£7.20)
       double day shift   workers *lose* £0.90 per week   (£3.60)
       day shift   workers *gain* £0.90 per week   (£3.60)

53

before the matter got to local conference, let alone York. That he did nothing of the kind makes it doubtful that the management ever had any but the most remote interest in the dockers' claim.

Secondly, it was well known amongst the stewards how Fine Tubes determined pay. They took a list of the ten largest employers in the district (including the dockyards) most of which were neither unionised nor federated. Averaging out the wages on this list, they paid the resulting amount. Thus the pay rise might not seem unreasonable, especially since, as already pointed out, there was a rush of pay increases locally in mid-July. But if, as the local union officials believed, these rises were to counter rising union membership, which in turn was inspired by the management's treatment of the strikers, then Fine Tubes end up provoking their own wage rise. In any case, the dockyard rise was not due to be implemented until the autumn, yet 9% of Barclay's 13% was to be backdated to within two weeks of the strike beginning. Thirdly, neither the dockyard workers nor the other local companies had made the very substantial concession of awarding staff status to its workers, nor had this ever been claimed by the unions.

A fourth, and important, point was that Barclay's award was itself in breach of the National Wage Agreement. As we have already seen, the only terms possible for a wage increase at this time were those of a productivity agreement—but no productivity agreement was ever cited by Fine Tubes management as a reason for the rise. Their claim that they wished to remain competitive with the dockyards ignored the fact that the dockyard rise was itself the result of a far-reaching reorganisation and productivity agreement, exactly the kind of agreement they had refused to discuss for over a year and a half.

That the whole business looked very much like another tactic to ensure that trade unionism did not return to Fine Tubes was recognised by Ron King, the local AUEW official. In a press statement immediately after the 'rise' he claimed that the strikers' claim was fully vindicated, and that the Fine Tubes strikers had clearly got something more than money at stake in this issue.

The strikers had a somewhat pyrrhic victory in August when the reference about the shift system reached York. The Employers upheld the unions' complaint, agreeing that the new system was implemented without consultation, and was therefore contrary to the National Procedure Agreement.

This confirmed the union officials' attitude that the rise satisfied the strikers' demand, since under the original shift system—now theoretically reinstated—the wage raise was all Barclay claimed it was. Thus it appeared the strike was won. The only problem was that the strikers were not there to reap the benefits.

7 The first six months

If the sackings at the end of June had moved the strikers to make long term plans, the pay rise at the end of July forced them to move fast to implement them, and determined efforts were made to obtain more than just local sympathy. A delegation had already been sent up to Bristol in the middle of the month and returned with a promise to 'black' from BAC/Rolls Royce aero industry workers, and more were sent out to the big industrial centres further north.

The local support was not always what one would have expected, indeed in some cases it was pathetic. A branch of 600 in the dockyards turned in £1.35 when the first collection was taken. Yet on the other side of the coin, the National Association of Local Government Officers, which is never in danger of being called a left-wing union, was amongst the first to promise its full moral support and sent £20 to the strike fund.

The dockers (to be distinguished from the naval dockyard workers) co-operated by blacking all deliveries to and from Fine Tubes, and the local British Road Service depot responded similarly. Even the local National Union of Railwaymen refused to handle more than the normal load from Fine Tubes, who had hitherto used the railways infrequently.

In the middle of August the Union of Postal Workers' local branch declared their support, and promised that they would not cross any picket lines, so for two days Fine Tubes did not get any mail. Unfortunately it could not last, as the postmen knew. The police warned the pickets they were liable to be charged under an act guaranteeing the freedom of movement of the Queen's mail, so thereafter the pickets always parted to let the postmen through.

It was during August that several delegations went out to various parts of the country, including Wales and the Midlands. One of the delegations arrived in South Wales in time to attend the annual miners' Gala and though they were disappointed to find that they could not address the gala from the platform, (it was too late to make arrangements), they were delighted when a little village pit band 'adopted' them, and led by a hastily improvised banner, the band and the delegation marched in the procession to much applause and cheering. To round it all off, the chairman's announcement from the platform, after outlining their struggle, called for a generous show of solidarity from the crowd, and the strikers went home with a three figure sum in spontaneous contributions.

Other delegations returned with promises of blacking support and similar financial success, so that by the end of August the strike fund was into four figures. By then, too, Fine Tubes' delivery traffic through the gate was down by forty per cent, and this was before the unions had made any national move to call for support.

The local success of the blacking was demonstrated by two of the more dramatic trials of strength which took place in the early days of the strike. A case of the right hand not knowing what the left was up to was brought to light in the first week in August. Amongst the first workers to support the black were the afore-mentioned Bristol aero workers. At the end of July, Mr David Cox, Labour MP for Bristol South, asked in Parliament if the Fine Tubes strike was having, or was likely to have any effect on the Concorde project. He was blandly assured by Mr David Rose, the Parliamentary Secretary to the Ministry of Technology, that the Concorde programme was in no way affected, nor likely to be. Two weeks later the following announcement by Bill Roberts (district secretary of the TGWU) was headlined in the local press:

'We have had an approach from the British Aircraft Corporation on the serious effect the Fine Tubes strike will have on the Concorde project.

The union has been asked to use its good offices to try to persuade its members to take the 'black' off the handling or use of Fine Tubes commodities, as a considerable amount of tubing is urgently required.

Our members in various parts of the country have refused to accede to this request until the employers at Fine Tubes agree to meet the full-time officers of the union and discuss the problem.'

The British Aircraft Corporation eventually found an alternative supplier, and it was the last that was heard of the problem until the following spring.

In Plymouth, further evidence of the effectiveness of the blacking operation came in a dramatic three-day saga at the beginning of September. Late in June, a three-ton crate had arrived for Fine Tubes at Plymouth dock. It had been unloaded, and though it was known to be an express delivery from the US, the dockers refused to move it; no drivers from BRS would collect it, nor would any crane driver lift it. Consequently the crate lay there for three months, until the middle of September, despite Barclay's cries that it was desperately needed.

In the second week in September, a Fine Tubes truck drove down under police escort to the dock gates. It was refused entry by the gatekeeper who locked the gates and walked off! The next day, the same convoy went down and this time was let in—only to find that access to the crate was blocked by two huge BRS trucks, whose drivers were nowhere to be found. A large mobile crane was 'requisitioned' from the other end of the dockyard. Being a contract-hire vehicle, the driver—a union member—came with it. Neither had been in the area for more than forty-eight hours and consequently the driver was unaware of the issues involved. He brought his crane across the dockyard and did not ask what it was all about until he arrived. When he did, a friendly docker explained things to him, despite police attempts to prevent him. After that, access to the crate was additionally blocked by a locked mobile crane, whose driver also had disappeared and was nowhere to be found. The third night the crate was eventually got out by supervisory staff and Fine Tubes scabs under police protection. But the episode had provided a good laugh at Barclay for the strikers and their supporters, and the drama was adequately documented in the local press.

Meanwhile, the management was doing everything in its power to break the strike. After twelve weeks there was concrete evidence from inside that their production was down by forty per cent. This figure corresponded with the detailed records kept by the 24-hour pickets, and appeared to be confirmed by the unprecedented overflowing storage space at the factory. They consistently advertised for workers in the local press with large and distinctive adverts long after they had stopped taking men on. Indeed, it became a favourite game of the pickets to ask a man, when he came up to the factory to apply for a job, if he had got it. After the end of July the answer was invariably 'no', even though the adverts kept appearing until the end of September, presumably as a propaganda measure.

During the summer a spate of anonymous letters, signed 'loyal worker', 'satisfied', 'hopeful', 'Britisher' (name and address supplied), and so forth, began to appear in the local paper, all emphasising that normal production was being operated, and that relations were a lot happier since the unions had left the factory. Other letters pointed out how much better paid they were than anyone else in the area, and how much overtime was being worked. (In fact there was firm evidence that there was none at all and the labour force was nowhere near pre-strike level either.) It should be pointed out that there is no evidence that Barclay was inspiring these letters.

One particularly vicious and absurd letter from 'loyal worker', claimed he dare not have his name published for fear of being beaten up. This inspired a maudlin and hypocritical editorial from the Plymouth *Western Evening Herald*:

'Has Plymouth really got to the stage where a person with a point of view is afraid to say who he is, for fear of being attacked by those who oppose his opinions but have already stated theirs?... This paper does not necessarily agree with the letters it publishes but it does so because it recognises every individual has a point of view and a right to express it...'

'Too often letters are received with the plea "Don't print my name and address or my landlord will throw me out", or something similar...'

'Too often' do they receive such letters! Perhaps. But it was significant that they chose to raise the issue in an editorial to attack strikers, rather than landlords.

Meanwhile the chessboard dance of unions and Employers' Federation officials continued at national level. In August, Moss Evans of the TGWU had urged the EEF to use their influence 'in recognition of their own member's violation of British standards of industrial relations', and included a strong hint of the strike spreading. When it was put to him by the EEF, Barclay refused outright, despite pressure from them and his local association, both of whom were worried about the undefined 'long term repercussions'. He was called to London and told to toe the line as his attitude might jeopardise the current delicate negotiations with the engineering unions for a new national procedure agreement, which the employers needed desperately at the time. Barclay ignored this, and claimed that since blacking was having no impact on him, he had no need to meet the unions. The EEF decided to meet them without him, to which Barclay agreed, expressing regret for any embarrassment he might be causing.

His popularity might have been low amongst his own national officials, but he found friends in strange places. Mr Victor Feather may have had some difficulty in finding sympathy with the strikers at Fine Tubes, but found no problem in sparing a little for the management in the second week of September when he rang Barclay to offer his services in settling the strike. Barclay turned him down rather sharply at the time, though Feather was to find him rather more eager some months later.

The meeting with the unions took place at York on October 8th, with the result that the unions declared that it was their last attempt to settle the issue peacefully, and that letters would go out across the country calling for 'appropriate action' in support of the strikers. They made some pointed references to Fine Tubes products used at GKN Sankey, Rolls Royce and the UK Atomic Energy Authority, and went out after reminding the employers of the Roberts-Arundel strike.

The only thing the EEF could think of doing was to refer the issue to the DEP at national level, which they did. Barclay welcomed the reintroduction of the DEP, saying that he believed his case would stand up to any scrutiny. However, by this time, mid-October, he was expressing concern over developments at the Atomic Energy plants at Windscale and Enfield where blacking had begun to bite. Further blacking at Hereford, in the GKN Sankey plant, worried him less. The reason for this was interesting, because it showed that Barclay knew the trade union movement well enough, whatever he thought of it. His unconcern was based on the knowledge that there was a large General and Municipal Union membership there, which he did not expect to support the blacking, and not surprisingly, he was right, though Hereford was to give him intermittent trouble in the future.

At this point, he felt secure in the knowledge that he was absolutely right in his conduct in the dispute, and confident that the new Tory government would not allow him to be seriously hurt. He thought that the blacking would accelerate the involvement of the DEP in the business, and that even if they failed, the Industrial Relations Bill, then going through Parliament, would put a stop to this nonsense for good.

Mike Bett of the EEF was not so sure though, and at the end of October he seriously urged Barclay to reconsider his attitude before it was too late. The inability of Fine Tubes' customers to find alternative suppliers, thought Bett, would result in increasing pressure on Barclay to talk to the unions, and a continuing refusal to do so would open him to wider criticism from all quarters, including his friends.

The re-entry of the DEP Conciliation Service into the picture gives an opportunity to examine a big story which broke in September. It appeared in the *Plymouth Post*, a monthly give-away paper consisting mainly of adverts. Nevertheless it managed to scoop the regular papers on a story of great importance to the area.

Readers were informed that the 'Plastic Carton Corporation' of America had planned to put up a factory in north Cornwall which would employ over 800 people. One of the DEP's many services to industry is that of giving advice and guidance to newcomers to an area. The advice the Plastic Carton Corporation received was—'don't pay the rates you planned. You can pay lower rates and still pay above average'.

Mr Peter Bissell, a director of the firm said: 'They told us the rates were too high and would result in other employers losing labour to the factory.' All the DEP had to say about this was: 'Any employer in any part of the country can ask for information. They can ask the advice of our experts of the effect of offering a certain rate.' It was clear that one desirable effect of a rate in the South West was that it kept the workers amongst the lowest paid in the country.

Harold Johnstone of the AUEW noted the ambiguity of the DEP's position when he commented, 'This is the Department which arbitrates for us in pay claims. How can they be unbiased when they give this kind of advice.' He had some reason to be annoyed. The twenty week strike at Centrax earlier in the year, over the issue of low pay, had been settled by DEP arbitration, and he had been the official in charge of the union's case.

The ensuing publicity embarrassed Mr Robert Carr somewhat, and caused him to announce a high level probe into why his Department gave such advice. As far as anyone knows, this probe never saw the light of day.

The strikers' ambiguous relationship with the Department began when they were all sacked. Since they were sacked, they could be considered unemployed. As such—having been sacked for industrial misconduct—they would have been entitled to unemployment benefit after six weeks, or so one would have thought. However, the Department decided that though they were sacked they were also on strike, and as such unavailable for work, therefore unentitled. So far, this would seem logical enough. However, although the factory was engaged in a dispute, they had no scruples about sending men to take the jobs of the sacked men who were still on strike and therefor could not get benefit. (The unions got the DEP to agree not to penalise any man who refused a job at Fine Tubes on principle.) If we assume the average dole payment for the men to be £10 per week, the Department was saving over £1500 per week on the 150 strikers alone. If Barclay employed another 50 locally unemployed men, the Department was saving £2000+ per week. Furthermore it is doubtful whether the strikers were included in the unemployment returns for the area.

The real idiocy of the situation however, was discovered by a Mr Ron Scott Glasby some six months later. Due to the increasing financial hardship, he dropped out of the strike on January 5th 1971, and signed on as available for work the same day. The following day he applied for a refresher course in his old job as a ship's radio officer. He was refused his claim for unemployment benefit while waiting for the course to begin, on the following grounds:

> 'Legally, if a person had been on strike and then signed for other work, even if he had been sacked while on strike, and had stopped drawing strike benefit, he would not be entitled until the strike ended.'

There was however, one very important and interesting exception to the rule, which was this: if the firm had sacked all the strikers, taken on fresh labour and *the plant was back to normal* (obviously in the Department's judgement), the Department might consider the strike at an end for its purposes.

Despite the fact that Glasby appealed against this decision at various levels, his final appeal in May, where he introduced this clause, was lost. So, as late as May 1971, it appears the DEP felt that it had sufficient evidence to be satisfied that Fine Tubes' production was *not* back to normal. Yet a month later, as we shall see, Barclay produced figures to show that Fine Tubes had had the best year in its history!

The strikers, having directed their attention 'up country' for most of the summer, turned the emphasis of their activities back to the locality. The autumn was spent trying to raise support amongst trade unionists in the Plymouth area, and they met with some success at a large meeting called at the end of October. Various ideas were discussed and the strikers, with full official backing, organised a city rally and demonstration at the beginning of December.

Ron King, district AUEW secretary, was the main speaker at the rally, which attracted over 250 people, making it one of the biggest demonstrations in Plymouth for years. For the first time King publicly accused Barclay of not merely having provoked the strike, but of having spent the previous six months, from January, in preparing for it, and using procedure as a means of stalling until he was ready.

The demonstration marked the end of the first six months of the strike, and afterwards in taking stock of the situation the strikers had some cause for satisfaction. Of the 150-odd strikers after the receipt of the dismissal letter, 130 remained, which meant that less people had left the strike than would have normally left the job had they remained at work, a cause for satisfaction in itself.

They had learned a lot too. From a somewhat complacent and haphazard beginning, they had developed an efficient system of picketing, a wide range of contacts across the country, a good fund-raising organisation, and some useful blacking, though not as much as they would have liked. On the debit side, they had been somewhat disillusioned by the apparent ineffectiveness of the official trade union movement, and were not entirely happy with the extent of general local support. Some aspects of blacking were giving them problems too, especially oil and steel. Quite early on they had effectively stopped all the major oil companies from dealing with Barclay, but the nature of the business was such that he continued to obtain supplies from small dealers, and through intermediaries. At one point he was having deliveries made to a small farm, and collecting it in his own tanker from there. His steel supplies too were continuing to arrive. This was to be a permanent source of trouble for the strikers, for they were never able to gain the co-operation of the notoriously right-wing steel union BISAKTA in the Osborn Steel group, Sheffield, who were his main, if not sole suppliers.

Nevertheless, on balance they were doing well. Barclay's deliveries of orders had been reduced from about four or five truck loads a week, down to around half a load. He had had to abandon large expansion plans, and his labour force was little more than half of that before the strike.

Indeed, about this time, Barclay appeared to be in very serious trouble when Rolls Royce cancelled an order for over 68,000 feet because of his 'inability to supply', and further orders were placed in jeopardy. He was also in trouble with Hawker Siddeley, and many smaller customers had stopped dealing with him altogether. When taken with his earlier lost orders from BAC and UKAEA, these were severe blows. It was a tight Christmas for the strikers, but the year closed with morale high. The only problem was that the plant was still producing.

8 Solidarity

The first winter of Conservative Government was a long hard one on the industrial relations front. After the bitter power workers' dispute before Christmas, there was the first national postal workers' strike from the middle of January. The power workers were only just held at bay in the final settlement in January, but the postal workers suffered one of the most total defeats of any union since the war. In the middle of that, the Ford workers went out for nine weeks, and restored the morale of the labour movement with a massive victory in April.

With all this going on, the few-score men and women in Plymouth were not getting a lot of attention from anyone, inside or outside the labour movement. This was unfortunate, because some attempt was being made to press for a Court of Inquiry at the highest level.

The *Sunday Independent*, a local newspaper, announced the first public airing of the idea by local union officials at the end of December and David Owen, a local MP, went to see the junior minister at the DEP, Paul Bryan, in January. Bryan came out flatly against such a suggestion and said in Parliament that such an inquiry was neither possible in present circumstances, nor would any benefit accrue from having one. The basis of his refusal was revealing to say the least. It was simply that the management was unwilling to co-operate. It would appear that firmness from the union, as in the power dispute, is blackmail, but from the management it is merely a 'refusal to co-operate'.

In February, however, Barclay received a blow to his hopes of Government intervention on his side when Owen managed to raise the issue in a parliamentary debate on the Industrial Relations Bill. After a sharp attack on the DEP, in which he suggested that it was actively helping the employer, he got Sir Geoffrey Howe, the Solicitor General, to admit that the strike would be considered as a 'fair strike', and worse, that secondary strikes in support, or in sympathy with it remain 'fair' under the proposed terms of the Act. This was a considerable psychological victory for the strikers, who were being consistently attacked as thugs and wreckers in the letters column of the local press. Barclay was livid, and at one point threatened, for some obscure reason, to sue Owen for his remarks in the House.

The year had apparently started well for Barclay when he was entertained by Vic Feather on the evening of January 4th. At this meeting Feather apparently told him that Jones and Scanlon wanted an end to the strike, and would soon advise the lifting of blacking and picketing. After presenting him with a signed copy of the *History of the TUC*, Feather allegedly told him that 'In your position I would have done exactly the same'.

The inclination to call the strike off was apparently confirmed when, at Central Conference in York, national officials reportedly remarked to that effect to the Federation officers. Barclay's information was good, for in March the TGWU Regional Secretary, Nethercott, came down with his national officer, Crispin, to talk to the strike committee about winding it up. The strikers were told that the National Executive were not convinced that the blacking was effective and, given the fall in numbers since the beginning of the year (there were eighty left by the end of March), they felt that the best thing was to pull out before the strike collapsed.

The strike committee argued vigorously that, firstly, it was not in the National Executive's hands to call the strike off, and secondly, they were so out of touch with what was going on that they were in no position to judge the effectiveness of the blacking or anything else. They produced the picket records showing the fall in deliveries in, and loads out, and they produced the head counts showing the fall in the numbers employed. But still the officers were not sure.

Both officers promised that they would back the men to the limit *if* they were in a position to take watertight evidence back to the National Executive. The strikers asked for a week to get it. The story of how that evidence was obtained, and its nature, must remain undivulged. Suffice it to say that one glance at it convinced Nethercott that the strike was not only biting, but was slowly being won.

In the middle of April, Nethercott issued a public statement pledging full support of the TGWU to the remaining 75 men on strike. This declaration heartened the strikers, as did the first sign that Barclay was rattled. This came when Crispin made another fruitless approach to the Employers' Federation for talks. The reply, passed back via the Federation, showed a reaction for the first time. Barclay accused the unions of trying to close the company down, which was surely an indirect admission that the union was having some impression.

There was an interesting practical test of a section of public opinion in the Plymouth local elections in April when Herman Welch, secretary of the strike committee, stood as a Labour candidate in the Whitleigh Ward. The ward is a mixed one, consisting in part of a large council estate, and also a large lower middle class suburb. The seat has changed hands several times since the war and hence is highly marginal. The 1971 election was undoubtedly the most vicious that the ward had seen, and Welch's Tory opponent made the most of being confronted with a 'striker' who was constantly referred to in the press as 'unemployed'. In a dirty campaign, the Tory consistently jibed at Welch as being the 'social security expert', and attacked him as a 'militant', a 'wrecker' and so forth. It was with some satisfaction that Welch took his council seat after having turned the previous Tory majority of 300-odd into a 500 majority for himself.

April and May were bad months altogether for Barclay, for the blacking campaign had reached one of his suppliers of raw tubing, Chesterfield Tube

Company, and though it had no immediate consequences, he continued to be in trouble in the aircraft industry, at Hawker Siddeley, Rolls Royce, and BAC, as well as at the UK Atomic Energy Authority.

The last week in May brought the situation at the Bristol plant of Rolls Royce to a head, and the strike back into the public eye. The workers there had been amongst the first to respond to the 'blacking' appeals. Soon after, the Secretary of State for the Ministry of Technology felt it necessary to announce that the Fine Tubes strike offered no threat to Concorde's development. Two weeks later, BAC in Bristol was pleading with the union to lift the blacking. The matter appeared to rest when the unions said nothing could be done.

However, on May 21st—ten months later—Rolls management at Patchway, Bristol, obtained a supply of Fine Tubes tubing which they knew was blacked. Their excuse was that they were in desperate need of it for the further production of Olympus and Pegasus engines, and this company was the only one with supplies available. Naturally, the storemen refused to handle the tubes. The following Monday, May 24th, the Rolls management threatened to dismiss all employees refusing to obey instructions by 7 am on Tuesday. 2,000 men walked out the moment the ultimatum was heard, and held a gate meeting where they rejected it outright. On Tuesday the workers reconfirmed their policy of blacking, and declared that if one worker was even disciplined there would be a full strike.

As soon as they heard of the trouble, the DEP needed no pressure to send conciliators post-haste to Patchway the very same day. They persuaded Rolls to lift the ultimatum and sit down to talks under their auspices. After eight hours, well into Tuesday evening, neither Rolls nor the unions would compromise, so Rolls reintroduced the ultimatum. This was due to expire 48 hours later on the Thursday night, despite the threat of 6,000 manual workers and 1,200 clerks to stop work if it was invoked.

The threat of such massive disruption in a major industry, and on such a prestige programme—especially after Rolls' collapse earlier that year—had more effect in moving the DEP and the local MP's towards the Fine Tubes strikers than anything the strikers had done since the strike began.

Anthony Wedgwood Benn, the local MP who watched the Concorde project like a guard dog, rushed into the picture on Wednesday and publicly invited Barclay to meet him with the view to discussing the possibility of talks. Surprisingly, Barclay agreed and called on Benn at his home in Bristol the following day, Thursday, and they spent about an hour together. What transpired can be guessed by the two statements Benn issued the same day. The first, within five minutes of Barclay's leaving the house said:

> 'The public should know that the danger to the Concorde programme and the new Rolls Royce Company stems directly from the attitude of Fine Tubes management... In my opinion, this dispute could be settled amicably within 24 hours were it not for the attitude being adopted by the Fine Tubes management.'

And from the second statement issued later:

> 'I invited Mr Barclay to join me urgently for round table talks with trade union leaders to seek a fair settlement of the official dispute that has now gone on for nearly a year... Mr Barclay made it clear that he was ready to speak to me alone, but not the union leaders... In my opinion, the behaviour of Fine Tubes, in refusing to enter any discussions with the trade unions, places the responsibility squarely upon them for the difficulties that have followed.'

The men in Plymouth had been saying that for nearly a year, but nobody had chosen to listen to them. Benn concluded his statement with a reference to the trouble at Rolls:

> 'The decision as to what action should be taken in Bristol and elsewhere must of course rest with the unions alone.'

As it turned out the unions allowed part of the load to be used: that part which was genuinely needed, on the understanding with the company that under no circumstances would any more Fine Tubes goods be used.

However 'storm-in-a-tea-cup' the issue may have been, its effect was to re-focus public attention on the Fine Tubes strike, to the extent that when the National Executive of the TGWU asked Vic Feather to call for a Court of Inquiry, Feather, much to Barclay's disgust, figured that the issue was sufficiently in the public eye to have to respond and issued an appeal to the Government in early June.

9 Public and private pressure

The result of the interview with Benn and his subsequent statement appeared to have shaken Barclay, for after a year of obstinate silence he felt obliged to accept the Inquiry proposal, publicly at least. Furthermore, he broke his press silence on the anniversary of the strike in a remarkable interview in which he began by justifying it:

'In the last year we thought that it would have added fuel to the flames, but I don't think that holds good any longer... The walkout was over a substantial wage increase and a closed shop... At the time when the claim was being pursued, they were signatories to a three-year national agreement which specifically precluded any application for a wage increase during its duration...it (*the claim*) was rejected by the (*York*) Conference on June 12th last year. It was rejected because of the three-year agreement. They were banned from submitting a wage claim.'

He also made the following claims, and produced a set of somewhat arguable accounts to support them. These showed firstly, that turnover for the year had increased by 28 per cent, and in the same period (June 1970–June 1971) sales figures had risen by 90 per cent. He further claimed that Fine Tubes was installing additional production capacity and was about to employ more workers. However, when he was asked if the factory was operated by non-union labour he replied. 'I don't know—I don't ask them. Membership is a matter for the individual.' He then went on to explain the labour relations set-up that currently existed in the plant.

Management/employee relations were handled by

a 'staff council' chaired by Barclay and consisting of twelve people 'elected' by the scabs on the shop floor. The council was registered by the DEP who arbitrated if 'failure to agree' resulted after three meetings. The final insult was the claim by the 'vice-chairman' that this council had 'negotiated' a 'salary' increase to operate from July 1st. Apart from his remarks about the 'staff council', Barclay's statement is inconsistent with all the evidence available.

Firstly, there are the closely observed records of the strike committee. The strikers' day-to-day sources of information were the 24-hour pickets posted at the only gates in front of the factory. Observations could also be made from the fields to the rear. The pickets had kept careful records, from the very early days of the strike, on the number, type, and size of loads being both delivered and sent out. A record had also been kept of the weekly head count of employees entering the plant on each shift. These records had shown a steady decline in consignments throughout the year. Observations from the rear of the factory confirmed that every available square foot of storage space was in full use. The head counts had shown that the total number of people employed, including office and maintenance staff, had fallen from over 311 to 246 a year later. Further checks showed that no overtime had been worked since the beginning of the strike. Given these figures alone, it is hard to see how production could have been maintained let alone doubled.

As to the question of additional production capacity, there are three reasons for suspecting the story as false. Firstly, the pickets knew well enough what kind of equipment would be used, and to the best of their very good knowledge none was taken in; secondly, a highly reliable source confirmed that Barclay's well-advanced negotiations with the DEP for a loan for expansion had been suddenly and inexplicably broken off by him earlier in the year; thirdly, there is Barclay's own statement at the Committee of Inquiry some four months later. An extract of this minute is interesting:

THE CHAIRMAN Have you any building plans that are likely to be started in the near future?

BARCLAY No sir.

THE CHAIRMAN Have you deferred anything that you intended to do?

BARCLAY Yes sir...and I say purely because of the state of the national economy.

THE CHAIRMAN You are employing 200 plus now: you are employing less than you employed before the walkout.

BARCLAY Yes sir.

There are three more points. Firstly, the DEP knew enough about Fine Tubes' affairs in the Scott Glasby case to successfully resist his appeal based on the supposition that the strike was having no effect. Secondly, the officers and executive of the TGWU were rapidly and wholeheartedly turned from a policy of defeatism to one of full support, on the basis of information obtained about the effect of blacking.

A third if minor point is Barclay's accusation—through the Federation—that the unions were trying to close the plant down. This was not the remark of a man confident of his soaring production figures. Finally, there is the question of the 'staff council': if any further proof was needed about the company's determination to refuse the union on principle in the six years prior to the strike, the wage rises negotiated by this spurious body proved it beyond doubt.

The unions' own recognition of the anniversary was hardly inspiring. It was no one's fault that the AUEW rules specified that strike pay could not be paid after the end of the 52nd week. It certainly was the responsibility of the union officials to inform its members of the progress of the strike, and encourage them to support a 'yes' vote in a union ballot to levy each member in the district two pence a week to compensate the loss. The first ballot was lost on a minute poll, and in an unprecedented move a second was held, but still the proposal was narrowly lost. It was the general opinion of those on strike that this was entirely due to the lack of energy of the officials.

The strikers' own celebration of their year of struggle took two principal forms. The first, on the day itself, June 15th, involved the strikers and fifty or more shop stewards from Rolls Royce Bristol and Coventry who joined the pickets' line for the day. There was a little scuffling with the police but no trouble. Barclay was greeted with a flank of Nazi salutes as he drove past.

This was but a token of things to come, for plans had been laid for a national day of picketing on July 30th. These proposals had already been backed somewhat belatedly by the two unions, as well as the local trades council and the Devon and Cornwall Federation of Trades Councils, and letters had been sent as far afield as Liverpool and Glasgow.

The men had expected a fair response from the replies they received, but nothing like the support that flowed in from 'up country' on the day, as coach loads of men drove in from all parts. In the end over 300 men came to demonstrate their solidarity and determination up and down the country.

To every silver lining there is a cloud however, and in this case it was the police. Sixty of the gentlemen appeared to supervise the celebrations and stir them up a little. As the strikers began handing leaflets out, and stopping the cars as they went in, appealing hopefully to their better nature for support—and before any hint of trouble had arisen—the police began shoving the pickets away from the gates. Some men asserted their legal right to picket. Then the trouble began, and within minutes the first arrest had been made. The police then encouraged scabs to drive through the gate at speed and the works bus was allowed to push through the pickets, and then bricks were hurled from inside the gates!

The incidents that were not provoked by the police were provoked by the scabs. One jabbed his fist through an open car window at the demonstrators. The vehicle was kicked, and two men leapt out swinging at the crowd; unfortunately the police got them back in one piece. Another hero drove his sports car through the crowd at somewhat more than walking pace, lost a headlight and radio aerial in the process, and rushed back with his fists flying after parking his car. By 10.30 nine people had been arrested, but the three people above were not amongst them!

Ron Nethercott, of the TGWU, said to the press later: 'This is the sort of thing we saw in fascist Germany before the war... At our last union festival in Bristol, the Chief Constable was our guest of honour—but I wouldn't have these blokes at the same table as me!' Strong condemnation indeed! Ron King, of the AEUW, said: 'This has been caused by the police—one or two constables in particular.' Finally, from Bill Roberts, the new TGWU district secretary: 'The police went out there with the intention of making it a field day.'

However, the picket demonstration was more successful than the strikers expected. After the scabs had gone into work and the men were arrested, the whole demonstration, except for a token picket, went back to a meeting at the AUEW offices where plans were reviewed for dealing with the arrests, and a second national picket day was organised for September. It was intended to get back up to Fine Tubes in time to meet the scabs coming out after work, but at dinnertime Barclay responded to requests from his terrified employees and police advice, and closed the factory for the afternoon, the scabs sneaking out at dinnertime, observed only by the token pickets and 60 policemen.

The consequences of the police behaviour bear some following up. After the protests of the union leaders, David Owen, the local MP, called for an inquiry 'by a very senior police officer from another part of the country', and restated his belief that a Committee of Inquiry would end the strike.

On union advice, several men laid charges against individual policemen and publicly expressed confidence in being able to identify their assailants. Consequently, the local *Sunday Independent* announced on the front page that the biggest police identification parade ever held would take place during the week. However, the following Wednesday some 'officers' had obviously had second thoughts, and after legal advice they refused to attend, so it was cancelled.

The first prosecutions of pickets were held on September 28th, when a Mr Peter Purchase from Bristol was found guilty of obstruction and fined £22. It took the magistrates an hour to find him guilty after police had given evidence of violent behaviour, despite the fact that it was not on the charge. He, like the others after him, gave notice of appeal. Next, Mr Cooper, also from Bristol, was found guilty of wilful damage to the works coach, despite evidence from two witnesses that he was thrown against it by the police. He was fined £102.50. Mr D. J. Hawkins from Exeter was charged with assault and insulting behaviour, and, in the face of evidence that, contrary to the charge, he was in fact beaten up, was fined a total of £73. Finally, Dave Edwards, a local man from the strike, was fined £32 with costs for insulting behaviour and obstruction. The only man to be found not guilty was a young teacher from Darlington, who was charged with assault against a Constable Smaldon, against whom several complaints had been made. Smaldon's evidence was so ludicrous that the magistrate was embarrassedly forced to dismiss the case for lack of sufficient evidence.

It is interesting to note that of the nine arrested, only five were charged, and of those five only four found guilty. The appeal results are even more interesting. Only two had their convictions upheld: one case (Purchase) had the fines withdrawn, and in the second (Cooper) the fine was halved. There seems little doubt that the local police and magistrates had been doing more than their duty.

On October 31st, the police announced the results of their Inquiry and sent out the following letter to all witnesses and complainants:

'I write with reference to your complaint against the police in connection with the incident which occurred outside the Fine Tubes factory at Plymouth on 30/7/71...Following a thorough investigation the file was sent to the Director of Public Prosecutions who has advised me that there is insufficient evidence to prosecute any police officer and in these circumstances I do not propose to take any further action in this matter.'

There was more in the same vein but the message is clear; the police had whitewashed themselves as usual. No action was to be taken. The fact that seven out of nine people had been arrested without grounds was just the police doing its daily job.

Barclay's summer was a dismal one. His confident expectations of an early finish to the strike at the beginning of the year had slipped away as an increasing number of customers began to feel the effects of the blacking. The news that the unions had not closed the strike, but were now actively endorsing it was a sharper blow than the news about the Industrial Relations Act. Feather's reluctant canvassing of an Inquiry must have been the last straw. He became convinced that he was the target of a left-wing conspiracy determined to destroy him at all costs, and throughout the summer he anxiously sent bunches of clippings to the Federation headquarters in London, not only from the local papers but from revolutionary papers like the *Socialist Worker*, the anarchists' *Freedom*, the *Morning Star*, and his favourite bogey, the *Western Worker*, put out by the local Tolpuddle group.

Despite his earlier public welcome of an Inquiry he seemed to be bending over backwards to stop it if he could. Early in July he went to London to see the chief conciliation officer of the DEP, Mr. Kerr. While there, with Federation officials present, he argued strongly that such an Inquiry would merely attract the publicity which the strikers had so far generally lacked, and raise the issue to national attention and importance which was what the unions wanted, and was the real reason for their request.

Early in August he again went to London, to meet Paul Bryan of the DEP, and made some bold claims to impress the junior minister. After claiming that he was producing 30 per cent more with 25 per cent less workers than before the strike, he went on to state categorically that the strike was being fostered and supported primarily by the International Socialists. Paul Bryan welcomed the company's resistance to the strike. Emboldened by this positive support, Barclay went on to refuse to take any part whatsoever in any Inquiry, or to consider taking back a single striker. Bryan answered that he would consider these points and reply as soon as possible.

Barclay came away without any definite answer but reasonably confident he had made his point, to the minister at least. Unfortunately for him, the permanent officials at the Department were not quite so gullible. On August 20th the senior conciliation officer, Mr Kerr, rang Barclay and told him the Inquiry was on, a decision which Barclay appears to have opposed strongly over the phone, since the following day he wrote a long, conciliatory letter to Kerr, outlining in more reasoned terms the basis of his opposition, which could be reduced to four points.

Firstly, such an Inquiry was unwarranted because there were no matters of great importance at risk. This of course, overlooked the domination of Fine Tubes products in the aircraft industry. Secondly, it was unjustified since the unions making the request were able to solve the problem themselves. (True, if to admit defeat was regarded as a solution.) Thirdly, it was unlikely to contribute towards a solution. This plea hardly reflects the confidence in his own case which he had so loudly expressed previously, for he must have known the unions would have certainly abided by any decision, and was here indicating that he would not accept a decision against him. His fourth point was that to grant such a request now would be to be seen to succumb to force as displayed on the national picket day, on July 30th. This was overlooking the unfortunate point that he had never made a positive move in his history at Fine Tubes without some sort of threat, except when it suited his tactics against the unions.

His plea did not cancel the Inquiry, but basically he was let off the hook when the Inquiry was publicly announced on September 1st. It was not a Court, but a Committee of Inquiry that was being set up. The difference was crucial, for whereas a Court can impose its decisions on the parties under threat of contempt, a Committee is a paper tiger, with nothing but a moral authority, and that was to be fatal.

The degree of co-operation he was likely to give to any Inquiry recommendations that did not give him one hundred per cent victory can be gauged by his mood at the beginning of September, still smarting from the decision of a couple of days previously. He wrote to the Employers' Federation with a view to taking legal action against the strike committee, and those who referred to them as the 'Fine Tubes' strike committee. The Federation officials dissuaded him from making a fool of himself in a letter which included the following:

'...There is nothing unlawful in these people describing themselves as the 'Fine Tubes' strike committee. If, however, as a committee they make any allegations against Fine Tubes, or issue any statement which reflects unfavourably on the firm, they would lay themselves open to a claim for damages ...assuming always of course that such statements or allegations were untrue.'

That of course was what everyone was about to find out. Barclay nevertheless continued to do everything in his power to stall the affair, insisting that 'duress' be lifted before the Inquiry. In this, he was publicly aided by a maudlin editorial in the local *Western Evening Herald* which virtually called for a total surrender of the strike by deliberately confusing a Committee of Inquiry with a Court. Nevertheless, the date of the Inquiry was set for October 6th, and Barclay had little option, under pressure from the Federation, but to acquiesce.

10 The Inquiry

The strikers' immediate response to the announcement of the Inquiry was to call off a second national picket day which had been planned for the middle of September, as a token of good will, but they rejected the whining hypocrisy of the local newspaper editor that they lay down their 'arms' and go into the Inquiry weaponless, and, despite some pressure, maintained blacking and the pickets.

A couple of days later the members of the Committee were announced. The chairman, Archibald Duncan Campbell, Professor of Applied Economics at Dundee, was an old government standby. He was chairman of several government wages councils, and economic consultant to the Secretary of State for Scotland. It appeared that he had hardly been out of Scotland, having previously held lectureships in Glasgow and Edinburgh; hardly a man of wide experience in the engineering industry.

The trade union member was Mr S. A. Roberts, recently retired from the presidency of the Boot and Shoe Operatives Union, and now a member of the Monopolies Commission. The Employers' Federation took the precaution of checking his suitability, and were greatly reassured when the president of the Footware Employers gave him the highest personal recommendation as a reasonable and co-operative man with whom he had the best personal relations.

The third gentleman was Mr John Rhodes for the employers, and the date set for the public hearing was October 7th. The main spokesmen for the union side were Crispin, national officer for the Power and Engineering Group of the TGWU, Johns, for the AUEW, and Harry Urwin, Assistant General Secretary of the TGWU.

The unions based their case against Barclay and Fine Tubes on Fine Tubes' lack of co-operation with the unions over a period of eight years prior to the strike; consistent and provocative breaches of agreement, both written and verbal (particularly in the last four years); the continuation of both, after the strike began, by refusing to talk; and further provocative acts. The unions did not consider that the strike was over money, or that at root it ever had been.

On the basis of a good deal of written and verbal evidence, tracing in detail the development of pre- and post-strike relations, Crispin, Johns and Urwin all asked the Committee to agree that the issue was about the fundamental right of trade unions to exist and operate in Fine Tubes. The one thing the unions did not do—and in my opinion it is unfortunate that they did not—was to challenge Barclay's evidence about his production figures, when they were in a position to do so.

Barclay treated the Committee with a disdain verging on contempt. After the unions had taken most of the morning stating their case, Barclay opened with:

> 'Fine Tubes has singularly little to say at this time, primarily because we do not feel we need to defend any of our actions. We are not here today, in any sense on the defensive... I submit we do not have a strike. We may have a dispute, but you cannot strike when you do not have an employer. Secondly, this is not a recognition dispute, and we would resist any attempts to make this a question of union recognition.'

This was hardly a useful start. He went on to base his position on the alleged breach of the 1968 package agreement by the unions when they submitted a wage claim not based on productivity. He justified his later actions by asserting it was his right, contravening no agreements or obligations on his part, to sack men on strike, whatever current practice may be. He also produced accounts, as he had the previous summer, which he claimed proved the ineffectiveness of the strike; these accounts did not tally with the strikers' own carefully-kept records.

Although his initial position was that he flatly refused to talk to the unions as there was nothing to talk about, the chairman eventually, after hard questioning, got him to commit himself to talking if the 'duress', i.e. blacking, was removed by the unions. He then maintained that that had always been his position. His whole attitude is best summed up by the following exchange after the chairman tried to find some basis for settlement:

BARCLAY Mr Chairman, forgive the question, but is it your intention to turn this Inquiry into a negotiating body in public?

THE CHAIRMAN It is not my intention to do that, certainly. May I ask you Mr Barclay if you have any proposals to remove yourself—or us—or the unions from the situation?

BARCLAY No sir.

THE CHAIRMAN None at all?

BARCLAY None.

THE CHAIRMAN Thank you!

The EEF was represented by Mr Ball, and its affiliated member, the West of England Employers' Association, by Mr West. Their contribution was significant largely by its absence. West said that he had tried to get talks going, but when Barclay would not co-operate there was nothing he could do. He advised him not to sack the men, but he had no power to prevent him from doing so. In short, he and his association were powerless.

Mr Ball for the EEF said much the same kind of thing. He made it quite clear that Barclay had acted within the rules of the Federation, and that he had the right to do as he did. Consequently, although the Federation might advise him to act differently, it had no choice but to support his right to act as he chose. In short, it too was as ineffective and powerless as the Association.

The Committee in its cross-examination seemed to be particularly interested in three main areas. Firstly, in the events of June 15th, on which it examined the stewards closely, and gave Chapman the personnel manager a very intensive grilling. Barclay overplayed his hand on this issue, right at the end of the Inquiry when he said in his closing submissions:

'You have the...task of determining where the truth lies... It is important...not so much because of the events of that day, but as to what it indicates lying behind and lying before.'

He said so little about so much, it was a measure of how important he considered it to be that his version of events should be accepted by the Committee.

The second area was the argument over the legitimacy of the 1969 claim. Although the union spokesman stressed that the initial claim was only an attempt to break through the obstinacy of Barclay to talk about money at all, he admitted that in the final analysis the claim was technically illegitimate in terms of the 1968 agreement, although they had reintroduced the issue of productivity in negotiations later.

The third area of interest was Barclay's attitude to talks. He was closely and vigorously questioned for about an hour by all three members of the Committee, to a degree nobody else had been. The result of this effort was the quote given earlier!

After closing submissions were made, the public hearing ended after having lasted only one of its two planned days.

The Inquiry published its report on November 24th, seven weeks after the hearings. Generally it favoured the unions' version of events. The first paragraph of its conclusion left no doubt that it concurred with them as to the roots of the strike:

'The immediate cause of the strike was the failure to resolve the pay claim which had been made eight months earlier... We think the company failed to keep as closely in touch with its shop stewards on matters of earnings and productivity as it could have done. This was, however, only the latest episode in what we regard as the real, underlying cause of the strike: namely the cumulation of a long period of poor industrial relations. We consider...the company...(has) missed apparent opportunities for desirable and useful consultations and negotiations with their trade union representatives.'

The report also said they found it impossible to establish the truth about the events of June 15th but goes on to say:

'...On the morning of June 15th...there co-existed a large group of people who were prepared to go on strike...and a small group who had not appreciated, despite recent experience and current approaches, that trouble could be on the way.

We are convinced the strike was predictable... We think there was enough evidence for the company if it had wished...to avoid...a strike, to have taken some initiative in approaching the unions for a meeting.'

There is then a sceptical note of Barclay's claim that he knew there was nothing amiss on the Monday, and the report goes on to comment sourly:

'The declared failure of management...to have appreciated the position points to some difficulties in collecting and interpreting evidence and/or weakness in communication at the plant.'

There is little question as to who they are favouring. As to the letter of dismissal, they found it 'peremptory' and 'damaging' and while regretting they had no choice but to agree that the company were within their rights, considered that too much of the letter and too little of the spirit of agreement was evident in the company's and employers' attitudes. They said clearly:

'We think that where strikes are official...the general practice of dismissal would be most damaging.'

Again they joined with the unions in considering the pay rise of July as a provocation:

We find it difficult to escape the conclusion that... (the) pay rise's timing and the manner of its making, could not do other than reflect adversely on those who had tried…to increase earnings.'

A similar remark was made about the 1969 increase for women, when Barclay was virtually called a liar:

'We understand…the Secretary of State did not announce equal pay until September 1969…*Even if* the company's reasons were as explained to us we think that this was badly done (my emphasis).'

As regards blacking and duress, Barclay could not win even when the Committee believed him. The national officers appeared unaware of the local success of the blacking campaign in the early summer of 1970, and of the Rolls Royce and BAC workers' solidarity which led to questions in Parliament that July, and to the pleas from BAC in August. Consequently, the Committee did not hear of it, and accepted that because no initiative was taken at national level over blacking, then there had been none taken anywhere until the middle of October.

Even the EEF did not seem to be in Barclay's confidence, as they appeared to have no knowledge of any blacking. At least they made no reference to it in two letters at the end of September, when they refused, on behalf of Barclay, to talk with the unions. These letters persuaded the Committee that there was no duress before October, and consequently that Barclay was not telling the whole truth when he said that he had always been prepared to talk if only he had not been subjected to duress. So the unions' failure to pursue Barclay's claims about productivity led to the curious position of the Committee accepting his figures which undermined his case on yet another point.

The EEF and the West of England Engineering Employers' Association also came in for criticism for being too legalistic in their approach to agreements, but the Committee seemed to recognise the basic ineffectiveness of the two organisations, and spent little time on them.

Although the unions' behaviour received almost no criticism, and the Committee made it clear that it had little faith in Barclay's version of any one event, its overall conclusions were pretty inept, even on the basis of its own accepted version of events. So, after accusing Barclay at least twice of serious provocation, it is rather strange that it placed the blame for 'a long period of poor industrial relations' on the attitudes of both management and unions, despite having produced no evidence of the unions' bad faith, nor accusing them of such.

One of the main points of the unions' case, accusing Fine Tubes of trying to get rid of them, was rejected by the Committee, simply because the company and the EEF had argued strongly that they were not. This raises questions about the unions' 'soft' tactics, because, although it was implicit in most of their evidence, they only posed the question, never pressing the issue to a direct accusation. This enabled the Committee to dodge the question, as they dodged the question of overall responsibility for the whole strike.

The conclusions were briefly that a settlement should provide conditions for establishing good industrial relations, but before this could be done the unions must agree to 'remove duress' and the company should agree to re-employ the remaining 49 strikers. Further arrangements for talks should be made under the auspices of the EEF as soon as possible, and the unions should suspend pickets and blacking while these were taking place. The end of the last paragraph is worth quoting for its total naïvety:

'However we leave these and other problems to those who negotiate on behalf of the unions and the company. As with most things in this dispute, if the wills to agree are there, agreement is virtually certain to be achieved.'

Such banality is almost beyond comprehension, and yet the unions have largely themselves to blame for the weakness of the recommended settlement.

The report feared that the strike could become a war of attrition if the two sides did not sit down to talk. From the evidence supplied the Committee had no reason whatsoever to believe that the workers had any chance in such a war (the union officials had contrary evidence but did not use it). It was clear that the report was a good deal more favourable to the unions than to Fine Tubes, but it was equally clear during the Inquiry that it was the unions who wanted a solution, not Barclay.

Given these factors, the 'soft' attitude of the unions and their apparent weakness meant that it was they who were going to have to 'give' in the face of the harder and apparently determined attitude of Barclay, regardless of justice or principle. It was a pragmatic solution offered by a Committee which had no way whatsoever of having its findings enforced, whatever their justice. Such results merely show the fatuousness of trade unionists expecting any fair dealing from such Committees.

11 Doldrums

Despite all the excitement of the Inquiry, the battle was still being pursued at ground level, and in October 1971 blacking at Hawker Siddeley was causing Barclay increasing concern, as well it might, since the Hatfield plant had switched suppliers and ceased dealing with Fine Tubes altogether. The Kingston plant had also managed, with difficulty, to find alternative sources, but on a temporary basis only. Other Hawker Siddeley plants were also approaching severe difficulties with their tube requirements for the Harrier jet, and at Kingston they were bending over backwards to disguise the fact from the stewards. By November, the management were driven to place a significant order with Fine Tubes, to be routed through an intermediary in Chester, so as to deceive the stewards. Within a week, stewards at the Yorkshire plant at Brough found out, and put a stop to that. Meanwhile, the EEF was desperately fending off the increasing flow of cries for help with words of patience as they awaited the results of the Inquiry.

The results of the Inquiry we already know. Barclay's reaction to them was, if anything, more negative and stubborn than that with which he met the appointment of the Inquiry. Shortly after publication of the report, he met with Federation officials in London to discuss it. There, he denounced the report as a 'worthless document', and again categorically refused to re-employ a single striker, specifically rejecting the recommendations of the penultimate paragraph, which called for the re-engagement of the remaining 49 on the basis of a time scale agreed with the unions.

Once again the Employers' Federation prevailed

upon him to at least meet the recommendation to face the union officials over a table, which he finally agreed to with reluctance, and only on the condition that he was free of all picketing and blacking.

The Federation conveyed Barclay's conditions to the unions in an attempt to start things moving, but privately their officials were beginning to have doubts about their continued support of Barclay. John West, of the West of England Association, wrote gloomily to Ball in London:

> 'I expect you have had a copy of Tom Barclay's notes on the Campbell report which puts the barometer needle for a successful conclusion to this affair in a very stormy part of the dial.'

Ball's carefully considered reply a fortnight later raised, cautiously but clearly, the question of the Employers' continued support:

> 'I believe before we get to a meeting with the unions, we should both consider our positions and that your member firm will not in fact be prepared to accept the suggested terms of settlement... We must consider whether we believe what the company has in mind amounts to similar provisions and whether we think that their proposals will constitute a reasonable compromise which your association and the Federation can both support.'

West was equally cautious and, again, gloomy when he suggested a waiting game:

> 'I feel we should await the outcome of your letter to the union officials, and if this produces a meeting, then once again I await the outcome of that... I would not wish to stir the pudding since in my heart I feel that tough Tom will suffer considerably as things proceed.'

Nevertheless, 'tough Tom' was allowed to continue to play the game as hard as he could without losing the support of the EEF.

At the start of the new year, the EEF informed the unions that Barclay was ready to agree to a meeting sometime in February, provided pickets and blacking were suspended as recommended by Campbell. When this was put to the strikers they were, to put it mildly, very wary, and refused to do anything until both National Executives reaffirmed support for the strike, and a firm date with Barclay was arrived at. This was finally obtained after his inevitable stalling, at the end of the month, and the strikers reluctantly suspended blacking and picketing in time for talks to start on February 16th.

Barclay seemed determined that nothing should be finalised in the one session, and that it should be adjourned to February 28th, which for him was a magic date. Indeed, it was not without significance for the whole British Labour movement, for on that date some of the most important provisions of the Industrial Relations Act came into force, including that section which made it illegal to take industrial action against a third party not involved in a dispute; in other words, blacking was outlawed. Barclay was back to pinning his hopes on the new Act, despite the warning of a year earlier.

He had worked out his tactics with the EEF, and had already, in January, decided to take the line that picketing had collapsed and blacking was ineffective without any action from the unions. This he duly pressed on the 16th, despite a private admission to the EEF a week earlier (and after the unions had issued suspension orders) that:

'...in a surprising number of places blacking continues. It would also appear that in some factories the stewards are determined to keep it up irrespective.'

No joint statement was issued after the first meeting, but a draft agreement was submitted to the unions. This was wholly unsatisfactory, and the second meeting at the end of the month left everyone back at the beginning, just as Barclay wanted. The document which the unions rejected read as follows:

(1) We recognise the trade unions' legitimate interest in seeking employment for their members with the company.

(2) The company's policy is to engage the highest calibre of employee from those applicants presenting themselves for employment.

(3) The company's policy is not to re-engage ex-employees unless there are exceptional circumstances.

(4) Notwithstanding (3) above, the company is prepared to consider the employment of any of those who went on strike in June 1970, and who have not already returned to work with the company. Wherever possible, such applicants shall be given preferential consideration.

(5) This must be however within the company's normal hiring procedure.'

This did not even correspond with the Inquiry recommendations: 'that the settlement should not be extended to cover more than the 49...people...on strike.' Furthermore, there was nothing indicating when, if ever, all the strikers would be re-employed, and to accept the programme as it stood would mean accepting the implications in items (3) and (4), that the company was doing the men a favour in giving them work. The fifth item, although apparently innocuous, was the one with the sting, because the company's normal hiring procedure was to take people from the Labour Exchange, and not to hire directly. (The address to apply to on their newspaper adverts at the beginning of the strike was that of the local employment exchange.) It also meant that the men had to undergo three months training—on training pay—before being put back on jobs they had worked at for several years.

On March 1st, Crispin went down to Plymouth to talk to the strikers and give a report on the discussions and their breakdown. In the course of his discussion with the strikers, he said that at least the programme offered a glimmer of hope and that, if the men were willing, he would persuade the National Executive to set a precedent and advance ten weeks strike pay, if they would accept the proposals of Barclay there and then. He was told bluntly that this was a sell-out and that he could not buy the strike for £50 per head—or at any other price. To his credit, he immediately backed down, and asked what the alternative was. He was told: 'Put back the black'. He dubiously agreed, and took that recommendation back with him to the National Executive.

Before Jack Jones made any public moves to support the strike he went to see Carr, the Minister of Employment and Productivity, on March 17th, and obtained a promise that he would 'look into it'. Carr then summoned Barclay to London on April 13th. Unfortunately, high politics once again interfered with events, and Carr was shifted to the Home Office early in April, to be replaced by Maurice Macmillan, who postponed the meeting while he dealt with simpler issues, like the pending national rail strike, and administering the new Industrial Relations Act.

Meanwhile, the national nature of the support for the strikers was once again demonstrated in London on March 12th, when the International Socialists organised a star-studded benefit concert in London. A couple of coaches were loaded with the strikers and their families to give them a weekend in London which ended at the concert in which several national figures gave their services free. Among them the East of Eden pop group and several well known folk singers including Alex Glasgow, Bobby Campbell, Trevor Hyett and Jake Thackery. The whole thing was compered by Bernadette Devlin, and needless to say, a good time was had by all and a large amount of money was raised. This was the first decent outing most of the families had had since the monotonous grind of the strike had begun.

After the fun was over, the strike committee began once again to travel over the country re-gathering the support the unions had suspended. In the absence of any official lead from the unions, and given the uncertain standing of anyone engaging in blacking in the light of the new Industrial Relations Act, it was both amazing and heartening to find that many workers all over the country were prepared to respond without question.

The first tour, of Merseyside, brought in support from Fords, Fisher Bendix, Standard Triumph, Dunlop and others. Barclay was quick to notice this; although he had no orders to any of these companies and his deliveries were not involved, he nevertheless was ready to use this activity against the unions as an excuse to avoid further talks. But he had bigger things on his mind than that.

On April 7th, he was unable to disguise the extent of his difficulties even after a three-month period free of blacking. 'Adjustments to the labour force are being made in line with current business,' he announced. In simple language 24 scabs were put out of the gate to seek their fortunes elsewhere, or in a word were made redundant. Among those to go was the senior metallurgical chemist and no less a stalwart than Mr Chapman, the personnel manager, who had stood by Barclay's version of events at the Inquiry: this was the reward of loyalty. Needless to say, the local press included only the smallest announcement of this triumph for the strikers, for which Barclay was duly grateful.

Other serious difficulties went unpublicised. At the end of April, Plessey at Swindon cancelled an order, and Rolls Royce stewards at Bristol announced that once again Fine Tubes was black, while further trouble was encountered in Hebburn at Pyro-Tenax when the stewards there informed the strikers of an order for Fine Tubes, before Barclay knew about it himself.

Early in May, Mr Maurice Macmillan, the new Minister of Employment, found time to take up the postponed meeting with him. This meeting proved once again the ineffectiveness of the use of government machinery, though Macmillan strongly attacked Barclay for his stubbornness and intractability and made it perfectly clear that he could expect no encouragement from him or the Government. He nevertheless had to write to the unions some three weeks later that 'there is no further action I can usefully take at this stage... I regret very much that it has not proved possible to resolve this long-standing dispute on the basis of the recommendations of the Committee of Inquiry.'

The strikers were disgusted, though by now hardly

surprised; as Herman Welch, strike committee secretary said, 'he seems capable of sorting out trade unions but not the management.' They were determined not to hang about any longer while the farce of talking to Barclay continued at their expense, and insisted on seeing their union leaders immediately, with a view to reinstating unequivocal, official, national action.

On 28th June, the strike committee went to Transport House for a meeting with the national officials. They were met outside, by a demonstration of support from miners, engineers, dockers and others, some of whom had come down from as far as South Wales. The meeting lasted over three hours, and more than two of them were spent persuading nervous officials to include the word 'black' in the joint statement, in the light of the new Act. The stewards came out reasonably happy: 'We got what we wanted, and more than we expected', said the vice-chairman of the strike committee, Frank Clarke, but they were wary of the value of the commitments they had got, and though pleased, would 'await future developments' before committing themselves to satisfaction.

What they had got was a commitment to restore full activity against Fine Tubes officially by the unions if the last round of talks, scheduled with Barclay on the 7th July, ended in failure. Nobody, not even the union officials, seriously expected to get any further than they had in February.

July 7th duly arrived and the meeting progressed through the now familiar sterile stages, with Barclay not moving from his stubborn and hostile stance of February, while the union officials desperately sought some sort of agreement to end the strike, which was by now a national embarrassment to them. The conclusion was inevitable, and reluctantly the officials declared an end to the official truce and announced the formal reintroduction of blacking.

12 The last stand

Two years, and nothing to show; that was the position the remaining 43 men and women faced at the branch meeting in the AUEW union hall on July 8th 1972. Most people would have reckoned it was time to cut their losses and accept an honourable defeat. The reason they did not was the same as that which had brought them out on strike: Barclay had got away with it again by breaking faith, as they saw it. In June 1970, he had got off at York, despite having deliberately flouted both domestic and national agreements—a view justified by the Inquiry report. In July 1972 he had again got off by equally deliberately disregarding the findings of the impartial and uninvolved Inquiry, as we have seen from his own words. The strikers had not spent two years out of work to let themselves be beaten by the same tactics that had brought them out in the first place. In any case, they could not believe, after such a public condemnation of Fine Tubes, that either the trade union movement or, in the long term, even the Government would let them go to the wall if the battle was renewed, so, unanimously, the battle was once again officially resumed.

Within a week their faith in their trade union comrades was endorsed, as the Coventry Rolls Royce plant added their renewed support to that previously pledged by the Bristol aircraft workers. Another visit to South Wales brought tremendous support from the miners who had themselves savoured the taste of victory earlier in the year. The support was not merely financial as previously, but moves were immediately begun to set up a local Fine Tubes support committee and they began their own efforts to stop the coalfield for a day in support of the

Plymouth men. Dockers at Avonmouth, Swansea, Liverpool, Middlesbrough and London pledged full support and also began to prepare for a token strike in protest. These perhaps over-ambitious plans however were soon lost in the dockers' larger battle that was already developing *vis-à-vis* the Industrial Relations Act.

On July 10, the secretary of the strike committee, Herman Welch, announced the possibility of the strikers using the Industrial Relations Act, despite the unions' opposition to it, to take Fine Tubes to court for unfair dismissal. On the following day, Barclay asked the Industrial Relations Court to send him the formal documents and explanatory notes necessary to make a complaint to the Court. Nothing transpired from either move; the strikers thought better of it when they saw the Act used against the dock leaders two weeks later, when the five were imprisoned at Pentonville. As for Barclay's move, he simply did not have a case, as he had been told consistently since the strike began, and as the unions knew when they re-opened blacking in July. Barclay's view, expressed to the EEF a week before he met the unions in July, that '...we will be threatened with their maximum efforts, including open illegal action, the latter can only mean they are nominating us as the crunch issue in their attack on the Industrial Relations Act...' was typical of his overblown sense of importance.

The dock strike not only removed Barclay's chance of starring on the stage of history, but also gave some indication, in a quiet way, of the respect the Fine Tubes strikers had gained across all sections of the labour movement for their ability to organise. The powerful and experienced London Dock Shop Stewards Committee asked the Plymouth strikers to supply it with their nationwide list of contacts, confidently expecting that it would be wider ranging than its own.

In the middle of July, a report in a West Midlands newspaper appeared to the effect that Fine Tubes' parent company was interested in buying up a Tube Investments factory in Walsall which was faced with closure. This was not without a certain irony, because that same summer a Fine Tubes subsidiary, 'Tube Sales', office was closed in Rugby since apparently it had little to sell.

At the end of the month David Owen, the local MP who had worked so hard to get the Inquiry called, and who was bitterly disappointed by its failure, went again to see Macmillan. Once more Macmillan stressed his desire for the DEP to act as peace-maker, but publicly admitted that in the last resort he had no powers whatsoever in the situation. (Slightly different to the situation as regards trade unionists, five of whom had just been imprisoned under his government's new Act.)

In the middle of August, a strike delegation went up to Sheffield to see the steel workers in an attempt to stop Fine Tubes' chief suppliers. It was not the first time they had been up there, and the previous autumn they had received, as they thought, a promise of co-operation from the BISAKTA local officer; but supplies of tubing had continued uninterrupted from the Osborn Steel Company. As it turned out, the actual orders for Fine Tubes were made at a subsidiary, Lowmoor Steel in Bradford, where they duly went. They failed to speak to any of the men there, due mainly to the obstruction of the BISAKTA officials in co-operation with the management.

A fortnight later nine of the Plymouth strikers returned to the Yorkshire Steel Plant and proceeded to picket the gate, and to the consternation of management and union officials alike, turned away over twenty trucks, including some carrying essential fluid gas supplies. The resulting contact with the stewards in the plant, who had been told nothing about the strikers' presence in the area by their officials, led to a mass meeting of the steel workers being called the next day. When the strikers had put their case, the workers unanimously voted to black all Fine Tubes' work.

Unfortunately, as soon as the Plymouth men returned home, the bureaucratic authority of the steel union officials asserted itself and on the basis of the Industrial Relations Act they dissuaded the men from effectively carrying out their pledge. BISAKTA, one of the most bureaucratic and conservative unions in the country was one of the few which had wanted to register under the Act, until brought to heel by the TUC.

The failure in Yorkshire was a blow to the strikers, but by no means a fatal one, as tube suppliers in Chesterfield renewed their support. An idea which had been tentatively put forward when the blacking resumed developed into a plan to call a national conference in Birmingham to gain the full support of all sections of the labour movement, and, hopefully, to organise one giant national effort which the official union organisation had hitherto seemed incapable of doing.

The strike committee sent out hundreds of letters inviting delegates to the Digbeth Civic Hall, Birmingham, on October 28th. Amongst those who did not accept the opportunity to attend were Jack Jones and Hugh Scanlon, although the engineers' Assistant General Secretary, Ernie Roberts, attended in a personal capacity. Amongst those who did accept were the UCS (Upper Clyde Shipbuilders) shop stewards and over 600 delegates from nearly 20 unions and 26 trades councils across the country.

Financially at least, the conference was a success; over £1000 was received in donations and around £150 was raised in a collection. The speeches were militant and the support unanimous, and the final resolution committed everyone to reinstating the blacking, and particularly urged the TGWU and AUEW to put their back into the effort officially.

The results of the conference over the next months, however, were patchy, and some of the promised support was, when it came to it, not put into practice. This is not to say that the conference had been of no use, for it proclaimed more clearly than any letter-writing or press articles could have done that the fight was on again with a vengeance, and the support gained was considerable. Nevertheless, it failed to build the final 'push' that the strikers had hoped for and which could have so easily broken Fine Tubes.

Barclay himself was doing some active support raising, and when, a few days before the conference, Lancashire Hawker Siddeley workers refused a load of special tubing not from Fine Tubes, but from the Pacific Tube Company of Los Angeles—another subsidiary of Fine Tubes' parent company, Superior Tubes, he offered to meet the stewards to explain his case. The men at Hawker Siddeley told him if he wanted to talk to trade unionists, he could start at Plymouth, a remark he didn't particularly appreciate.

By the end of November, a delegation on a nation-wide tour of the major industrial areas obtained further blacking support, and when Christmas came around the local Labour club helped organise a Christmas party for the 52 children of the strikers' families.

On December 3rd, the *Sunday Independent*, a local paper which had dealt marginally more sympathetically with the strikers than the two local dailies, published a half-page feature under the headline 'The Pilgrim Factories', which managed to devote over half its space to Fine Tubes without a single reference to the strike. Among other things, Barclay claimed that he was employing over 300 people, a figure which on the strikers' evidence was only 225. Elsewhere in the press he publicised the installation of new equipment, including furnaces which had in fact been installed in 1968.

Clearly everything was being done by the local 'establishment' to help the Plymouth people forget about the inconvenient bunch of people who kept hanging around the gate all day. Indeed a few days later a delegation from the local trades council, which had not always been as active as it might have been, went to see the manager of the local employment exchange to remind him of his earlier pledge not to penalise men refusing jobs at Fine Tubes on principle, but did not get full satisfaction.

The new year began with new moves on the parliamentary front, when fourteen trade union MP's met the leaders of the strike committee in Westminster and promised to harrass Macmillan, still Minister at the DEP, through questions and procedural motions. A fortnight later, five of the MP's met Macmillan, who promised to look into the possibility of reconvening the Committee of Inquiry, though as usual little was to come of this activity.

Back in the real world, in Plymouth, the strikers were preparing another national picket day for March 19th. The plan was to raise a picket of around three or four hundred to meet the scabs as they came in at 7 am, picket till 9 am, return to the town to have a meeting, and then at midday have a demonstration through the town. It was a lavish programme, and ambitious, since it required at least 250 trade unionists to be at the gate by 7 am on Monday. However, it turned out to be quite modest, in view of the turnout.

Nearly 700 people, all trade unionists, travelled through the night to reach the gates of Fine Tubes that Monday morning; some, from Scotland, had spent the best part of Sunday in their coaches as well. The factory itself was hardly visible behind the forest of union banners from every part of the country. There were strong contingents from the Welsh miners, as well as the London docks and the Bristol and Midland Rolls Royce plants. There was also a very large contingent from the Plymouth City Police (estimates vary from three to five hundred). Strong suspicions that they were not there from any sense of solidarity with the strikers were rapidly confirmed when they formed a passage three or four deep on either side to let the scabs through, refusing to stop them to enable one man to exercise the right of speaking to them. When the scabs began to drive through the crowd at speed, the only police reaction was to arrest people who reeled against them as a result. Nevertheless, the local 'gestapo', as Ron Nethercott had dubbed them two years earlier, had taken warning from the row their behaviour had caused on that occasion, and though there were individual examples of police thuggery, there was none of the organised brutality of July 1970.

After two and a half hours, during which many of the scab labour force gathered behind the hedges in a field half a mile up the road, the pickets went into town for a conference, which filled the ABC Cinema. The conference was addressed by, amongst others, Ron Nethercott, Ron King, and Paul Foot. But some of the most interesting speeches came from the floor, almost all of which were highly critical of the trade union officials, and one of the biggest receptions was given to an old London printer who asked why the union leaders were not at the picket, and suggested that what was needed was a demonstration outside the national AUEW and TGWU offices to get the leaders 'off their asses'. There was no doubt that the feeling of the conference was that had the union leaders the will to do so, the strike could be finished in a week. Nevertheless, in the midst of the enthusiasm and militancy, Frank Clarke, the vice-chairman of the strike committee dropped a hint in closing that the strikers were weary of the long struggle, as he said they would be glad to go back to a job for the rest. The conference then broke up, and the delegates re-formed outside to show Plymouth the largest workers' demonstration it had ever seen.

The picket/conference/demonstration was not the only activity supporting the strikers that day, for up in Bradford, a forty-man picket was outside the Lowmoor Steel Works. These were local Yorkshiremen disgusted with the scabby behaviour of the steel workers. In Plymouth the workers at Arrow Hart, a near neighbour of Fine Tubes, stopped for an hour in support of their brothers.

The day's activities brought a renewed wave of support for the strikers across the country, and the Bristol Rolls Royce workers who had consistently supported the strike decided to black work from the Derby plant, where the convenors had with equal consistency refused to black Fine Tubes products because it might affect their jobs. The Coventry Rolls Royce plant joined in this pressure on Derby, when the workers there decided not to send any work to Derby. It was hoped the resulting publicity would get things moving again at the 'higher' levels if nothing else.

Meanwhile, the strike committee secretary, Herman

Welch, who was also a local councillor, began to receive a spate of threatening phone calls and anonymous letters, as did to a lesser extent Frank Clarke. These were of similar character to the letters which had appeared in the local press in the summer and autumn of 1970. One letter warned, 'Remember, physical violence can affect you or your family... You can be attacked quite easily so ... denounce Monday's attacks (*the national picket*) as hooliganism, or be prepared to suffer it yourself.' The letter was not signed, and so there was no concrete evidence that it came from one of the scabs inside Fine Tubes but no one amongst the strikers doubted it; they had their own knowledge of some of them.

The rush of support after March 19th was unfortunately not maintained. Although some of the Rolls plants made strenuous efforts, it was eventually not possible to maintain their boycott of Derby, for a number of internal reasons. Other pledges, including, at last, the cessation of Barclay's ammonia supplies, came too late, for as Frank Clarke had warned, the strikers were weary, mentally and physically.

On June 1st, the strikers met to consider the situation; they were only a fortnight away from their third anniversary on strike. Their hope that the March 19th activities would stimulate a rapid end had not been met, and though they were hitting Fine Tubes probably harder than at any time since the Inquiry, the question was no longer how the strike was affecting Barclay, but how it was affecting them. 14 people had left the strike since the previous July, leaving only 31 still out. The end of the summer would almost certainly see the strikers down to a handful. It was already difficult to maintain regular pickets, though it was being done one way and another. It was with tremendous reluctance, though not without a sense of relief, that they decided to quit while they were still together. For the sake of the full three years, they decided to pull out on their third anniversary, June 15th. One thing was certain; they had earned a place in the annals of labour as the longest strike in British history.

13 Final Betrayal

Their troubles even then were not entirely over; as Paul Foot was to say in *Socialist Worker*, there remained the 'Final Betrayal'. If the strike was lost, the strikers were not cowed, at least not by Barclay.

The strikers decided to write to all those who had supported them so loyally and consistently throughout the years, and agreed on a long statement to be sent out. The first part thanked them for their support, and then went on to analyse the reason for their defeat as follows:

'We owe it to you briefly to set out what we feel are the main reasons for our apparent lack of success.

First, of course, we received no assistance from those employers who profess their support for trade unionism. The Engineering Employers' Association, although they pretended that they did not approve of Fine Tubes' anti-union stand, did nothing whatsoever to back up that disapproval. A single threat from them could have finished Barclay off, but they preferred to shelve their so-called support for trade unionism in solidarity with a wildcat employer.

Secondly, the capitalist press was at all times unconcerned about our case at Fine Tubes. We had to put up with all kinds of nonsense and vitriol from that quarter. Only the left-wing press, in particular the *Morning Star*, the *Socialist Worker* and the *Workers' Press* gave regular coverage to our case and our campaigns.

In several crucial cases we came across shop stewards and convenors who for reasons best known to themselves did not black Fine Tubes:

in particular, Rolls Royce, Derby; Osborn Steels group, Bradford; Henry Wiggins, Hereford; UKAEA; BAC of Preston—all 100 per cent organised firms, who thus left open crucial loopholes through which Barclay operated.

We are bound to say that although the strike has been official from June 15th 1970, and although official blacking notices have been sent out again and again, by the two unions involved, our cause has not been pursued by the official union machinery with the persistence and dispatch for which we had hoped. We cannot believe that the two biggest trade unions in the country have not got it in their power to break a small anti-trade-union employer, whose workers had voted for recognition.

In more than one case, the unions officially stood aside while stewards and conveners agreed to black Fine Tubes. "There is nothing more we can do", we were told time and time again, when effective and determined leadership from the top could have ensured the total blacking of Fine Tubes.'

The letter concluded after warning that other employers might be encouraged to provoke recognition disputes by the failure of the strike:

'We must be vigilant to ensure the failure of such attempts. We must tighten our organisations, demand more from our officials and executives and strengthen the left-wing press... Each and every one of us intends to take jobs in factories in this area, and to do all in our power to strengthen trade unionism in this part of the world.'

The proposed letter, as can be seen, was pretty powerful stuff. It summarised concisely, and in unequivocal terms, everything that the strikers had learned in the preceding three years. The weakness and hypocrisy of the employer and government agencies and the national press was shown, and the alternatives, which from experience they had found useful, spelled out. Unfortunately they dealt with similar frankness and honesty with the role of their own trade union organisations, and this was not to the union leaders' liking. (The full text of this letter is included at the end of the book as an appendix.)

Shortly after their decision to pull out, the four original stewards, Jack McQuade, Frank Clarke, Herman Welch and Dick Williams, went down to London to settle the winding-up details of the strike with their union officials. There were six officials there, one from each level of the unions concerned; Tom Crispin of the TGWU and Bill John of the AUEW were the national officials; Ron Nethercott and Vic Evans, TGWU and AUEW respectively from the regional level; and Ron Webber and Ron King, TGWU and AUEW local officials.

A copy of the letter had already been forwarded to them, and they opened the meeting by agreeing at once with the sentiments in the letter, but went on to express concern about the strikers' already none too rosy prospects of getting fresh work in the area worsening if the letter went out. They were particularly worried about the identification with the left press.

For four hours, the stewards argued for their document, pointing out that it and its implications had been discussed in depth, and accepted unanimously by those concerned, the strikers, who were big enough to look after their interests without any help from the officials: they had had to for the last three years, after all.

As the argument progressed it became clear that the issue at stake was not the strikers' future welfare, but the officials' prestige, and that of the unions, and the officials wanted all but the innocuous opening paragraphs cut right out. Nevertheless, the stewards stuck doggedly to their point until Crispin played his ace card.

The Finance and General Purposes Committee of the TGWU had agreed to pay each striker £130 to tide them over after the strike; however it had yet to be ratified by the National Executive, which was to meet in a few days. Crispin pointed out that they might not feel much inclined to do so if they saw themselves so attacked and there was the chance that they might reverse the decision.

That was it: the boot in no uncertain terms. The 31 strikers had fought for three years on an issue of principle, and now they were to be robbed at the last of the money which had been promised them, if they maintained those principles. It was more than they could take—the money meant so much to them in their personal financial situations. It would help clear the slate to start their domestic lives again. Three years, and then this. What was the use? In despair and disgust the strike meeting in Plymouth the next day voted twenty-seven to four to accept the required cuts, insisting only on the retention of the last sentence: 'Each and every one of us intends to take jobs in factories in this area, and to do all in our power to strengthen trade unionism in this area.' Even this the officials thought unwise—but they let it go. They had got what they wanted.

Paul Foot, in *Socialist Worker*, on the day of the official ending, June 15th 1973, wrote that the strike had ended not with a bang, but a whimper. Perhaps —but his publication of the original document helped a little to turn the whimper into a growl. Perhaps in one way it was a fitting ending. For three years the men and women had fought with only the half-hearted support of the official unions, and in the end it was a left-wing paper that had allowed them to say what they wanted, and finally have the last laugh on them. As the *Morning Star* said: 'While the day is sad, it is also tinged with a certain pride that men of the South West could hold out so long for union rights.'

14 The strikers' experience

The 31 men and women, now ex-strikers, kept their word. A month after it ended almost all had found jobs in the area with remarkably little trouble, and of the local factories, only Tecalemit appear to have operated a 'blacklist'. What kind of people have their new employers hired? Certainly they are very different from those Barclay sacked three years previously, as the people concerned will readily admit.

One view of themselves that the strikers would fiercely resist is that of their being 'heroes'. To regard them in that light would be to miss one of the central points of the strike, which is that in the last analysis, any self-respecting worker can and will fight an employer who pushes them too far, even in the West Country. They feel it is important to emphasise that if they, with so little previous experience, can build up the fighting organisation that they proved to be able to do, then there is an example for all workers in backward and underdeveloped areas to learn from and to use.

Though proud of their ordinariness at the beginning, they avoid taking it too far, for they, more than most, appreciate the value of experience and knowledge. Their disgust with the official trade unions stems in part from the realisation that these working class organisations which ought to be the 'bankers' of such experience, basically left them to learn the hard way, on their own. Their political attitudes too have developed considerably. The significance of the fact that the fullest and most unqualified support came from the so-called 'red troublemakers' has not escaped them.

Any suspicion that they themselves were 'a tightly knit group of politically motivated men', was completely squashed, if somewhat patronisingly, by a Mr John Goss, who made an independent inquiry into the strike a year after it had begun. This gentleman, a local management consultant, was not himself without political motivation, having been a Tory candidate in the 1970 election. His independent inquiry, as he was to find, suffered from one major defect: its unavoidable conclusion that the strikers had an honest case. His conclusion, published in 1971, was as follows:

'During the course of these interviews, I formed the opinion, from my experience, that the strikers were a good type of working person forced to fight for their case, and probably willing to continue to do so to the point of desperation.'

The Tory intolerance for integrity, honesty and foresight resulted in his being dropped by his constituency soon after the appearance of the report.

The survey covered 54 people and gave the following personal details. 44 were men and 10 women. 35 were between ages 25–45, and all but a couple were married. 28 of them had 54 children between them. 20 of them were local men and two were foreigners. Of the rest, 32, many were ex-servicemen who had married and settled locally—indeed several were navy pensioners. Only 17 had been at the firm less than two years, the majority, 23, had been there between two and five years, and 14 had over five years employment. None of these men were exactly casual workers, with 75% having over two years service. 21 had had regular military service, and 28 had previous long service in one job.

These were figures that indicated to Mr Goss 'a good type of working person'. This patronising phrase seemed to please many of the strikers, perhaps because it maintained that they were still 'respectable', and not 'troublemakers' as the local press tried to present them. The long service records of the large majority of the men show that they are capable of settling and of being satisfied without making 'unreasonable' demands. Patronisation aside, these figures demonstrate conclusively the 'steady' and reliable nature of the men and women on strike.

Details of union membership and activity are interesting, showing that of the 54, 28 first joined the union only when they came to Fine Tubes, and a mere 20 considered themselves active to the extent of even attending branch meetings. Bearing in mind that these people were the hard core of what was to become the longest engineering strike in English history, and was already over a year old, these were remarkably modest levels of pre-strike activity. Even more remarkable, though not mentioned by Goss, was the fact that several of these people did not walk out in the November 1969 trouble, and one even stayed in on June 15th, 1970, only coming out the next day.

The personal toll on the strikers was considerable over the years. For every one who left through lack of enthusiasm and increasing disillusion as the strike dragged on, another was forced out of it against his will, either through economic or domestic pressures. Two for instance were faced with court orders to pay large maintenance arrears to ex-wives or going to prison, and consequently had to find jobs. One striker indeed ended up in Exeter jail because he could not afford to pay a £10 fine for having no TV licence. Such was his independence that he did not mention this to the strike committee, who only found out about it through a local newspaper article. Needless to say they paid the fine and he was released immediately.

One of the largest single reasons for men dropping out was the pressure of unsympathetic wives and families. This kind of pressure was particularly strong on ex-naval men who had no families of their own in the area. One man, subjected to hostile domestic attitudes, nevertheless refused to abandon his brothers until eventually the contradictions of his situation became unbearable and he suffered a nervous collapse, which was an extreme example of a common problem. However there are at least four men who, when faced with the final choice, chose the strike before their wives, and are now separated as a result. There were other wives who, after initially being in opposition, developed with their husbands a wider awareness of the implications of the strike, and were at the end active supporters of their menfolk.

For all the strikers, the experience was valuable politically and socially. Many, previously no more than Labour voters—if that—have used the time on their hands to develop a wider understanding of society well beyond the immediate issues of the strike, and all of those who lasted out learned a great deal. When they began, none of them were very much aware of any of the 'left' political groups, and certainly not sympathetic to them. No concept of class struggle existed, nor did any sense of being a part of a wider working class movement. In short, they were apolitical, non-militant (ie 'reasonable') voting fodder, well integrated into the concensus society.

The picture by the end of the strike was very different. Their involvement in the union was self-evident, as was their militancy. They are now all clearly aware of the 'left' groups, and though in one or two cases a little wary of their interest in the strike, are undoubtedly sympathetic to their ideas to the point in some cases of joining them. All are conscious of the nature and concept of class struggle and feel very much involved in the national working class movement. In short, they are now politically aware, militant (ie 'unreasonable') people, to a greater or lesser extent disillusioned with the 'just society' they were sold for so long.

15 The company and its allies

The unfortunate and unavoidable truth about the Fine Tubes strike is that the company won. Barclay, by dint of good luck and tactics, is now able to operate free of all ties with the unions. But at what cost? That is something that is unlikely to be known for a long time, if ever, though all the available evidence points strongly to that price being high.

His constant claims of not merely maintained but increased production and sales were always open to strong doubt in the face of overloaded storage space, basic forty hour week working, and the reduced traffic through his gates. They became even more suspect in the light of abandoned expansion plans and the redundancies of 1972. As for the accounts which he referred to in support of his claims, it is interesting to note that he has not published such accounts since April 1970 (up to the time of writing) although they were always previously made available annually.

If the price was really high, who was paying it? Not Barclay: he was only a hired manager, so it can only have been the parent company across the Atlantic, Superior Tubes of Pennsylvania.

Remarkably little is known about this firm, not least because it appears to have an obsession for secrecy. It is a privately owned company, based near Philadelphia, with some twenty subsidiaries, mainly in the USA. No information about its financial affairs is published, and sources which would normally supply such information report it as unavailable. This indicates a more than usual degree of secrecy on the company's part. Several interesting though unrelated items of information have been unearthed however, and the reader can make of them what he will. Firstly, one of the sudsidiary companies,

Lantel Inc, is a holding company for another which runs WDCA-TV channel 20, in no less a city than Washington DC. The significance lies in the enormous political influence needed to obtain such a broadcasting licence in the capital city, which must obviously lie with the parent company.

Secondly, several senior directors in the group appear to be of Italian extraction, though that is hardly surprising, given the Italian influence in Philadelphia. Thirdly, though union relations do not appear notable in either direction, not all plants are organised, and 'decertification' elections have been held successfully in at least one plant. Decertification is a legal provision in US Labour law for voting out existing union representation, which has to be 'voted in' in the first place. It is unusual for such elections to take place, and usually involves the employers' encouragement.

Thus we have a small international company based near Philadelphia with strong political connections, an unusual taste for secrecy, significant Italian-American influence and a possible distaste for unions. This company is backing a reactionary manager in England in an effort to shift the unions from the factory at apparently almost any price. 'Why?' is a question that cannot be answered specifically, and speculation could be libellous.

Barclay himself has always been consistent in his public declarations that he has nothing against trade unions in principle. But, as the Scottish workers at Peterhead will testify, his antipathy to them in practice precedes his arrival at Plymouth by a good many years, and was certainly a constant factor throughout the pre-strike period at Fine Tubes, as the exchange with Jack McQuade in 1968 showed. At best, it would seem that he has always adopted a very hard line in his dealings with unions, and this was probably an important qualification for his getting the job in the first place.

The possibility that he was actually hired with a long term brief to be rid of the unions must be considered, particularly as he arrived so soon after the company's first strike. A new manager might be expected, whatever his personal views, to make some attempt to restore industrial relations to a better footing, rather than continually exacerbate the situation as he did, unless he had been given such a brief. The question 'why' once again returns, and still there is no satisfactory answer, and yet his behaviour hardly makes sense in any other light.

Nevertheless, even with such a brief and such backers, he could never have got away with it without a great deal of co-operation, or at least tolerance, from institutions and organisations in this country which might have been expected to bring some pressure on him to compromise. This particularly applies to the Engineering Employers' Federation and the Department of Employment and Productivity.

It would be naïve to expect the Employers' Federation to be impartial in an industrial dispute, even when their member is totally in the wrong, but there is little doubt that they were embarrassed by Barclay almost from the start, when they were presented with the *fait accompli* of the sackings. Their authority, and hence their credibility as spokesmen for the employers, was consistently undermined in front of the unions as Barclay's silence continued in spite of their pressure. Indeed their patience was pushed nearly to breaking-point after the Inquiry (at which they had looked rather ineffectual), when Barclay refused point blank to accept the proposals offered.

The question arises as to why they failed to do anything about him, even expel him if nothing else was possible. In part at least, it is possible that they were more frightened about what he would do without their influence than about what he was already doing while nominally within it. It is true that they were able to exercise some restraint upon some of his more outrageous ideas, when they knew about them. For example, Barclay was seriously considering taking legal action against the strike committee in September 1971 for their continuing reference to themselves as the 'Fine Tubes' strike committee. As this was just before the Committee of Inquiry was due to be held, the EEF moved rapidly to prevent him doing anything so stupid which would prejudice

114

an already shaky case. They similarly dissuaded him from dragging Vic Feather into the Inquiry. This arose when Barclay wanted to publicise the content of their January discussions.

All through the dispute, the EEF's attitude seemed to be based on doing as little as possible in the hope that the problem would disappear. By the time they realised that it would not, it was far too late to bring Barclay to heel. As we have seen, there were signs that they were getting exasperated just before the Inquiry, as well as later. Barclay must have had an idea that they would drop him if they got the chance, because he appears to have been careful enough to allow them to dissuade him from some of his more provocative tactics. These of course may have been in any case only random shots to keep the EEF on the hop. He knew well how to play their patience to the limit, while being careful not to step beyond it.

The Department of Employment and Productivity was a different case altogether. Their attitude was based on the broader political considerations of their masters. Their ineffectiveness was based on a cynical Tory tactic to aggravate the industrial situation. The Department's Conciliation Service had been virtually put in mothballs soon after the Tories came to power, as a contribution to the raising of strike figures, thus providing further justification for their Industrial Relations Bill.

Clearly, despite Macmillan's sincere regrets, the one institution that the Government could have used to help settle the strike was never seriously activated, apart from the calling of the Inquiry. Even the Inquiry was set up only as a Committee and not a Court as soon as the minister saw that a Court would have to use its powers. The Committee was a convenient sop to noisy elements like David Owen and the unions, while avoiding the necessity of having to act on the results.

With two of the major organisations in industrial relations staying neutral when according to their own rules they should have been pressuring him, Barclay was free to face the unions unencumbered and, if he needed it, he had a major ally locally, the press.

The *Western Morning News* and the *Western Evening Herald* could hardly have served Barclay better had he owned them himself. They played up his statements and muted his difficulties, while burying anything but unfavourable reports of the strikers' activity completely.

Some indication of the kind of treatment the strikers could expect can be gathered from an incident early in 1971. When Sir Geoffrey Howe had made his remarks in Parliament about Fine Tubes being a fair strike, the first edition of the *Evening Herald,* which was sold mainly in the Plymouth hinterland, rural Devon and Cornwall, reported it alright, but by the time the city edition appeared, the one the people of Plymouth read, it had vanished, apparently because someone had told the editor it was libellous or inaccurate. It will be remembered that Barclay threatened to sue MP David Owen for his remarks in the House when the statement was made.

With such support and friends, it is hardly surprising that Barclay got away with so much, but need he have won? He was, after all, not fighting a handful of local men and women but two national organisations, three million strong.

16 The unions: realism or cowardice?

The failure of the Fine Tubes strike was, at bottom, the failure of the two biggest battalions of the working class—the Transport and General Workers Union and the Amalgamated Union of Engineering Workers—to hold their own against one small American firm. This humiliating defeat was not based on the unions' physical inability to fight and win; after all, Ford Motor Company was brought to its knees, as was the Government on several occasions while the strike was on.

The cause of the defeat was basically a lack of will on the part of the official union leadership. The problem was not that Fine Tubes was too big or too powerful; rather it was the reverse, that it was too small and too isolated. It was an embarrassment at a time when the trade union movement was facing a battle for its traditional rights, against a Government that was determined to 'put it in its place'.

Once the strike was well under way it became fairly clear that the only likely way of winning the strike, short of Barclay being sacked, which became increasingly improbable, was to close the plant down. Purely in terms of trade union strength, this was entirely feasible at any time they chose, but it presented difficulties in a wider context. On one front the trade unions, including the two involved, had elected to fight the new Industrial Relations Act by trying to deny two of its main premises: that the unions had too much power, and that that power was used irresponsibly. In other words, they decided to a large extent to fight on ground of the enemy's choosing. Instead of emphasising their strength and their right to use it for the working class, they preferred to lay greater stress on their 'responsibility and reasonableness'. As the slogan later was to become, they were out to show that with them 'common sense will prevail'.

It would have been very easy for the Tories to use such a closure of Fine Tubes as a major propaganda weapon against the unions to prove precisely those premises, and the unions concerned knew it.

A second point was that for the larger part of the three years, unemployment nationally was rising alarmingly. It would have been a great political bonus for the Tories to have the unions contributing to that rise in an area with a traditionally above-average unemployment rate and, furthermore, discouraging new investment in the area.

The third point was tied up with the fates of Rolls Royce and Concorde. Rolls Royce went bankrupt early in 1971, and in flagrant contradiction of its declared policy the Government bailed it out, thus saving thousands of jobs. Thorough blacking by Rolls workers across the country of the only company capable of producing a particular component would undoubtedly have resulted, at least in the short term, in several hundred lay-offs. Again, an awkward and embarrassing situation for the unions who would have been held responsible, not only by the Tory press and their masters, but probably by many of their members, whom the leaders were trying, not always successfully, to mobilise against the Industrial Relations Act. The same situation existed as regards Concorde, which provided work for thousands within the West Country itself. This programme was in any case under Government scrutiny, and its future appeared to hang in the balance for some time. Again, the unions would have been presented as tipping this balance against continuation of the project if they held it up with a blacking campaign.

None of this is offered as an excuse for the trade union officials' soft line on Fine Tubes, but it does follow from a fundamental political decision, completely beyond the Fine Tubes issue. The question as to whether the official trade union tactics and strategy used to fight the Industrial Relations Bill/Act, unemployment and the Tory Government were correct or not lies beyond the scope of this book. All that can be said is that the nature of those tactics and strategies in the economic conditions and political atmosphere of the time led inevitably to the failure to support the men at Fine Tubes to the full, given the probable nature of the victory—closure of the firm.

Indeed it was exactly this kind of official attitude which brought to the British labour movement a new concept of industrial struggle in the summer of 1971. This was of course the factory occupation which was first used in the Upper Clyde shipyards. This, which was always a rank-and-file tactic, was to prove extremely effective against the wave of closures which were threatening to take place. Unfortunately the Fine Tubes strike was already a year old by this time, and you cannot decide to turn a strike into an occupation after you have already started.

However, even the most radical national leadership would find it difficult, if not impossible, to organise and run a strike from the top, even if it was structured to do so, and the TGWU is certainly not. As one of the most decentralised, as well as the biggest union in the country, it is clear that the National Executive depends heavily on the reports of its local officials. The content and tenor of these, especially in a small strike, are all they have to act upon. Consequently, their action is likely to correspond to the attitudes of these officials.

If we can judge from the line that Crispin was pursuing with the employers, on behalf of the National Executive, both in talks and at the Inquiry, the local officials were not presenting the strike as an issue of trade union rights and principles, but simply as a money dispute exacerbated by a stubborn employer. It is easy to brand such officials as scabs and reactionaries, but especially in the context of the South West the explanation is less sinister, if not less unflattering. Given the level of trade union consciousness and activity in the area generally and the TGWU's policy of using only local men as officers, it is unlikely that such men are going to do anything other than reflect the general local level of consciousness. (This TGWU policy changed after the strike began, but still applied at the time under discussion.) It is axiomatic that militancy starts at the bottom, and not at the top; unfortunately, in Plymouth, it stopped at the local officials. Given such shortcomings of both officials and environment, it is clear that the kind of local 'official'-backed struggle that ultimately won the Roberts-Arundel strike at Stockport was never a serious proposition.

Another problematic element of the strike was that of timing. In this respect the strikers appear to have been consistently unlucky. The strike occurred three days before the election of a Government pledged to limit trade union power. This alone would have guaranteed that, given its size and apparent unimportance, it was not likely to receive much high-level union attention as the leaders took in the new national situation. It may even be this factor which explains why the national officials did not get around to even attempting a national blacking campaign till October. The Inquiry results too, and the abortive discussions, took place when the attention of the labour movement was directed elsewhere, towards the struggles of the power workers, the miners and the builders. In fact throughout the whole period the struggle at Fine Tubes was denied the status of being the *cause celebre* of the labour movement, either official or unofficial, overshadowed as it was continuously by larger and more spectacular struggles.

Having subjected both national and local officials to fairly sharp criticism, justified in the face of the evidence, there remains the inescapable fact that the main union involved, the TGWU, backed the men financially for three years. To those sceptics who would point out that it cost them nothing but their members' money, one can only point out that while true, even this support would almost certainly have been denied the strikers ten, or even five years previously. It would not have been too difficult to sell the strike out completely; certainly much easier than another union found the betrayal of the Pilkingtons workers.

Given this much financial security, Fine Tubes

120

would seem to have offered an excellent opportunity for the 'unofficial' rank-and-file movement to show the union officials how to win a strike. It cannot be denied that very often they did just that, and it was undoubtedly the tens of thousands of pounds raised on the shop floors to support the delegation activities that kept the strike alive as long as it did. Nevertheless, the rank-and-file movement showed, in the last analysis, that it too was incapable of winning the Fine Tubes strike, despite its main weapon, blacking.

The reason for this lies in part in the nature of Fine Tubes' production process. Both its supplies and products are not continuous deliveries but batch supplies. This caused one of the major problems of the strike, which was that though the delegations constantly received guarantees of blacking, very often the goods still got through. The reason was that Barclay frequently used intermediaries to confuse the source or destination of goods. Thus, as soon as he heard that a delegation had received support from one of his suppliers of customers, he usually had sufficient stocks to take time to find another supplier or set up an intermediary.

The strike committee soon found that they totally lacked the enormous resources required to maintain the kind of checks needed to counter this operation. The only thing that could have conceivably done so was the official union machinery. This would seem to indicate that the unofficial movement, by its fragmented and localised nature cannot, at least in a situation like Fine Tubes, act as a complete substitute for the official trade unions.

With this conclusion, we arrive at one of the main lessons that the strikers themselves pointed out in their abortive final statement, that 'We must tighten our organisations and demand more from our officials and executives...' In other words, the unions must be made to fight for, rather than talk on behalf of their members; their material resources remain an essential supplement to the struggle of labour militants who cannot afford to discount or abandon them.

The question remains, what did the strikers prove

with their three-year marathon of hardship, poverty and courage. If Ron Nethercott was right in July 1970 when he staked the future of trade unionism in the South West on the outcome of the Fine Tubes strike, then surely its future is very bleak now? No. Barclay remains in business, successfully rid of trade unionism, true. But at what cost? Three years of constant harassment, cancelled orders and under-capacity production is a high price in any terms, and it is highly improbable that there are many employers in the area who would willingly embark upon such a round even a quarter as long, even if they could afford to.

If that is the case, and the price of non-trade unionism is beyond most employers, then the men and women of Fine Tubes Ltd who set that price have not fought in vain, and, as so often in trade union history, those who follow will reap the benefit.

Postscript

As this book goes to press, some four months after the end of the strike, some interesting and highly relevant developments have taken place, both in Fine Tubes and in the local unions.

At the Fine Tubes factory, around a hundred scabs, after failing to get a further wage increase through their 'staff council' in August, left the company's employ. Among them were four or five of the 'hard core' of a dozen or so militant anti-trade-unionists who had formed the backbone of the scab labour force (insofar as it can be said to have had one!). Of these, at least two have sought and found work in the naval dockyard, where the union writ has been extremely strong in the last few years.

Meanwhile, though some replacement labour does seem to have been recruited, there are now less than 100 employed on the shop floor, as against over 200 when the strike was called.

A second point of interest is the apparent discontinuation of the management's practice of informing their employees of their orders in hand. According to an ex-scab, these were regularly displayed on the works notice-board throughout the strike. Indeed, not only has this practice been discontinued, but, according to the same source, all enquiries in that area are now brushed aside somewhat brusquely.

All this would seem to bear out the contentions of the strikers that the management was not revealing its true position to anyone during the strike, including the Government.

Nevertheless the Government, through its control of Rolls Royce, certainly appears to have done all in its power to support the company. For example, it has recently emerged that the Bristol Rolls Royce management made a payment of over £70,000 to Fine Tubes for an order, eighteen months in advance of the due date of delivery: this amounts to a tax-free and interest-free loan to an anti-union employer from public funds.

On the local trade union front, it appears that the lessons of the strike have finally penetrated the official machinery. With the withdrawal of three of the local TGWU officials for health and personal reasons, the new officials have received positive instructions that in the event of any future 'Fine Tubes-type' situation developing they are to put their full energy into bringing it to a rapid and successful conclusion.

Thus it appears with increasing clarity that if the strikers themselves did not win an outright victory, they have certainly inflicted a mortal wound on both their ex-employers and on the flabby official trade unionism that has hitherto existed in the area.

Appendix

This is the full text of the letter the strikers wanted to send out: after the union officials' objections, only the first six paragraphs were actually sent.

FINE TUBES STRIKE COMMITTEE
c/o 65 Bretonside
Plymouth

June, 1973

Dear Brothers and Sisters,

We are writing to tell you that we have decided on June the 15th to call off the strike at Fine Tubes Limited, Plymouth, which will have lasted for exactly three years.

The decision has been agreed by the thirty-one remaining strikers. It has been made with great regret, but we all feel that it is better to end the strike when we are still an organised body rather than watch the strikers disintegrate.

Our first concern is to thank all of you and your organisations for the help you have given us over the past three years. We have all learnt a lot about the working class movement in this country in that time, but most of all we have learnt that solidarity is not a dream; it is a reality which has been expressed to us in many different ways. We have travelled in delegations right across the country, and in almost every town and city we have found organised workers who have come to our assistance. Branch after branch of different unions, shop stewards committees, joint sites committees and individual rank-and-file trade unionists have dipped into their pockets to help keep this strike going over such a long period.

We have had help too, in even more direct ways.

On two occasions we have staged mass pickets outside the factory gates. Several hundred trade unionists came both times to demonstrate their solidarity, and both demonstrations put new heart into the strikers. In October 1972 we also organised a conference in Birmingham which was attended by more than six hundred delegates. In particular, we would like to thank those trade unionists from the South West, allegedly such a 'backward' area, who have helped us so readily.

To each and every one of you and your members who welcomed us, listened to our case and helped us to sustain the struggle, we say: Thank You, and if necessary we would certainly do the same for you.

In spite of all this solidarity, however, the strike has failed in its main object, and a stubbornly anti-union boss is still operating. We owe it to you briefly to set out what we feel are the main reasons for our apparent lack of success.

First, of course, we received no assistance from those employers who profess their support for trade unionism. The Engineering Employers' Federation, although they pretended that they did not approve of Fine Tubes anti-union stand, did nothing whatever to back up that disapproval. A single threat from them could have finished Barclay off, but they preferred to shelve their so-called support for trade-unionism in solidarity with a wildcat employer. Secondly, the capitalist press was at all times unconcerned about our case at Fine Tubes. We have had to put up with all kinds of nonsense and vitriol from that quarter, especially from the local press. Only the left-wing press, in particular the *Morning Star*, *Socialist Worker* and *Worker's Press*, gave regular coverage to our case and our campaigns. Thirdly, we have learnt that the familiar device of the 'committee of inquiry' has to be regarded with the greatest possible suspicion. In our case, a 'committee of inquiry' found out that the employer was entirely wrong, and then recommended a 'compromise' which gave the employer almost everything he asked for.

All this, of course, might have been expected. What

has surprised and worried us most of all, however, are the weaknesses in our own movement which have contributed towards the defeat of the strike. In several cases, we came across shop stewards and convenors for reasons best known to themselves who did not black Fine Tubes, in particular Rolls Royce, Derby; Osborn Steels group of Bradford and Henry Wiggins, Hereford; UKAEA; BAC of Preston, 100% organised firms, and thus left open the crucial loopholes through which Barclay has operated. In others, internal and local jealousies between the established lay leadership of the union have taken precedence over solidarity. The result in these cases has been disarray, which has been blamed on other factors, such as the alleged 'backwardness' of the South West area.

Finally there has been the attitude of many of our union leaders and officials, including the TUC.

We are bound to say that although the strike has been official from the 15th June, 1970, and although official blacking notices have been sent out again and again by the two unions involved (the AUEW and the TGWU), our cause has not been pursued by the official union machinery with the persistence and dispatch for which we had hoped. We cannot believe that the two biggest trade unions in the country have not got it in their power to break a small non-union employer, whose workers had voted to strike for recognition. In more than one case, the unions officially stood aside while stewards and convenors refused to black Fine Tubes. 'There is nothing more that we can do', union officials told us again and again, when effective and determined leadership from the top could have ensured the total blacking of Fine Tubes.

Employers who think like Barclay should take warning of our efforts. Fine Tubes were the most progressive company in the area (not wage wise) but are now struggling to survive, having suffered severe financial losses. Protected as they are by the Industrial Relations Act, they will seek to 'cash in' by provoking further recognition struggles in carefully-picked areas. *We must be vigilant to ensure the failure of any such attempts.* We must tighten our organisations, demand more from our officials and executives and strengthen the left-wing press so that, when the next Fine Tubes locks out its workers, the trade union movement's response is immediate and invincible.

All these lessons, however, merely strengthen our enthusiasm and gratitude for the solidarity we have experienced over the past three years. Each and every one of us intends to take jobs in factories in this area and to do all in our power to strengthen trade unionism in this part of the world.

It is hoped that the ECs of both unions, despite our decision, will issue instructions that the blacking remains on Fine Tubes indefinitely.

Yours fraternally,
C. Williams,
    Secretary, Fine Tubes strike committee
H. Welch,
    Chairman, Fine Tubes strike committee